Books 3
Range

Books & Range 3

THE MANY-STORIED CABIN

Greg Hill, Alaska Librarian

Illustrated by Jamie Smith

The Library Foundation, Inc. | Fairbanks, Alaska

Published by Hill of Books Publications.

© 2017 by Greg Hill

Hill, Greg

Books Range III : The Many-Storied Cabin / by Greg Hill, Alaska
Librarian.

1.   American newspapers--Sections, columns, etc.
            Smith, Jamie.
            Title
III.   PN 4874. H54 .A25 2017
814.54

Cover illustration by Jamie Smith

Contents

Backward vs. Foreword . . . . *vii*

Gutenberg, Gust, and Rare Book Libraries. 1

Hifalutin Dogberries and Abstract Nouns 4

Dogs, Dr. Seuss, and the Moral Molecule 7

OMG!, Recency, and Soccer 19

Hyphenites, Assonance, and Monkeyshines 22

Careful Words, Commas, and CIA Style. 28

Demonyms, Pedants, and Reading for Fun 31

Life-Long Learning, Degorging, and Zeugmas. . . . 34

Feckless Similes and P.G. Wodehouse 37

Tyrannio the Rapscallion Librarian 40

Phantoms, Idiots, and Restrooms 43

Bad Boys and Girls, Who's Who, and Mr. Toilet. . . 46

Torture, Webster's, and That That. 49

Poprocks, Paraprosdokians, and Kindness 52

Pronouns, Pseudonyms, and the Curiosolites. . . . 64

Guys Ropes, Guy Fawlkes, and Guys Read 79

Pronouncing, Murals, and Building Vocabularies . . 91

Little Words, Ngrams, and Smiley Faces 94

Lazy Men, Ugly Men, and Human Books 97

Love, Mistakes, and Marilyn Monroe 100

Admiral Wrangell, Word-Lists, and Venery 103

Grammar, Justice, and Yahoos. 106

Poor Judgment, Nasty Metaphors, and Intolerance . 109

Fat Ladies, Receipts vs Recipes, and Love Talk . . 118

Bubbles, Words, and Colors 121

Holes, Moons, and Tea Parties. 124

Dashes, Dots, and Librarians. 127

Nonplussed Emojis Not My Fault 130

Old Books, Old Librarians, and Literary Iceland . . 133

Petting, Sweating, and Spizzarinctum 136

Yogi, Gene, and Norman 139

Messiness, Disgust, and Reproduction 142

OMG, Dord, and Circumflex Perplexion 148

Rudeness, Cakewalks, and Library Fines. 151

Grammar, Style, and Nonpologies 154

Prisons, Libraries and Bug-eating Coaches. 157

Cheecks, Civility, and Logofocos 160

Tigernuts, Shopping Lists, and Animal Skin 163

Khipus, Goldfish, and Memorable Mimosas 166

Flirting, Swearing, and Classy Curses 169

Flowers, Fireflies, and Frequentives 172

Obnubilate Zinio, Y'all 175

Gobblefunk, Gold Cards, and Blind Boy Groot . . 178

Synesthesia, Misophonia, and Argle-Bargle 181

Fine, Criticism, and Ms. Mutch 184

Songs, Styles, and Rackslappers 187

Obscure Sorrows, Crosswords, and Amyloids . . . 190

Words, Colors, and OZ 193

Political Women, Dog Whistles, and Lady Bird . . 196

Skimming, Scanning, and Illiteracy 199

Deep Reading, Lizard Feet, and Touch Cookies . . 202

Backward vs. Foreword

"Forward" is defined a number of ways in the American Heritage Dictionary (my favorite browsing dictionary). These include "lacking restraint or modesty," "ardently inclined," and deviating radically from convention." While these little essays are to some degree guilty on all counts, the first one in the AHD's list, "At near, or belonging to the front or forepart," is probably most suitable to this occasion.

Their second definition, "Located ahead or in advance: *kept her eye on the forward horizon*," gave me pause, though. The book you hold is clearly oriented towards the past, reviewing columns that appeared in the Fairbanks Daily News Miner years ago. I'm indebted to that worthy publication for their willingness to print my semi-library-related columns every week for going on twenty-seven years. Of course, I've done that gratis, for public servants shouldn't even appear to profit unduly from their positions, and any and all proceeds from the sale of this book goes straight to the Fairbanks Library Foundation. So it's been a win-win-win.

Those who are familiar with my broad views on spelling and primitive typing skills know that none of this would have been possible without the careful oversight and gentle corrections made by a bevy of friends, co-workers, and one wife who has read them all. You know who you are, and I'm forever in your debt, really and truly.

A fascination in words, language, and how humans read and write, have long been the grist for this mill. Our language's convoluted history, the way our words accrete meaning, even where writing came from hold endless vistas to explore for some of us. That particular interest was certainly shared with a certain library volunteer who was an exemplary worker — kind and efficient, curious and sweet-natured, dedicated and quick-witted. And it's to her memory that this book is dedicated.

—Greg Hill, April 2017

Books Range 3

Gutenberg, Gust, and Rare Book Libraries

....

Old Johann Fust was something else. He underwrote Gutenberg's printshop with two loans in 1450 and 1452 totaling 1,600 guilders, but three years later, when Gutenberg's Bibles were almost finished, Fust sued for 2,026 guilders and won all Gutenburg's Bibles and equipment. Some historians view Fust as the beneficent enabler of the creation of print technology, yet it's suspicious how Gutenberg wasn't anticipating Fust's foreclosure, nor how quickly Fust took possession of Gutenberg's equipment and soon began printing Bibles with the assistance of Gutenberg's former apprentice, one Peter Schoeffer, who a few years later married Fust's daughter. Fust and Schoeffer sold the Bibles for 40 guilders each, about 2,200 modern Euros, passing them off as hand-made.

The full story's unknown, and much of what we "know" is unreliable. For example, many people assume that German goldsmith Johann Gutenberg invented the printing press. MIT's "Inventor of the Week Archive," describes how Gutenberg created "a device that would make it possible to print texts using moveable blocks of letters and graphics. These, used with paper, ink, and a press, would make it possible to print books much faster and more cheaply than ever before."

However, Gutenberg didn't invent the press, paper, or special ink; others did all that. He's been credited with finding a suitable metal alloy for producing durable molds for reproducing fonts of sturdy type that can be taken apart and re-used. Now a librarian and physicist from Princeton have proven that Gutenberg didn't even do that.

Paul Needham is the head of Princeton's Scheide Library and a noted rare book scholar. Though located on the Princeton campus, the thirty-by-thirty foot Gothic-style Scheide Library is actually the personal property of millionaire book-collector William H. Scheide's. Princeton lets Scheide's library adjoin their main library because it's among the world's greatest book collections, and Scheide gives their students access. William T. Scheide, H's grandfather, began the collection with a first edition of Michael Faraday's "Chemical History of a Candle." A much later edition's on the Noel Wien Library shelves, and it's an entertaining read.

William T., a colleague of John D. Rockefeller, acquired many rare books, but his son and grandson extended the collection dramatically. In fact, the Scheides have their own chapter in Nicholas Basbanes' excellent "A Gentle Madness: Bibliophiles, Bibliomanes, and the Eternal Passion for Books," also owned by our library. Need a First Folio of Shakespeare's works? The Scheide Library's got several, along with an original of the Declaration of Independence, Beethoven's autographed sketchbook, and the big four in Bibles: a Gutenberg, and a "36-Line," a "Mentelin," and a "1462" printed by Furst and Schoeffer.

The "36-Line Bible" is also known as the Bamburg Bible, after Bamberg, Germany, its probable place of origin. It was printed in 1458, about when Gutenberg died, and is the second printed Bible. Some experts think Gutenberg printed it, too. Johann Mentelin was another German printer whose Bible came out in 1460. William H. just acquired the Mentelin Bible recently for somewhere "in the seven figures." All these Bibles are extremely rare; only two other people have ever owned all four simultaneously: King George III and the second Earl Spencer, Princess Di's relative. According to a **www.Princeton.edu** article, Needham and his associate, physicist Blaise Aguera y Arcas have shown that instead of re-using the same pieces of metal type to print the various pages of his Bible,

Gutenberg may have "used an earlier technology that involves casting letters in molds of sand — molds that could not be re-used." The sand was very fine, fooling generations of scholars, but modern computers and applied mathematics showed that the individual letters that should have been identical all varied. "Nobody is going to say that this was made by crude technology," Needham pointed out, saying "On the page it looks better than books today."

Furst and Schoeffer's 1462 Bible, utilized red ink. Furst presented copies to the King of France, pretending it was hand-made, but the ruse was detected. Worse, the identical letters in each book led to suspicion of witchcraft, and the red ink was thought to be blood.

As another American Librarian, Lawrence Powell, put it, "We are the children of a technological age... Printing is no longer the only way of reproducing books. Reading them, however, has not changed."

Hifalutin Dogberries and Abstract Nouns

There's a lot to be said for reading The Economist. Besides in-depth, authoritative reporting, its writers and editors employ richer vocabularies and more formal grammar than low-brow rags like Newsweek and Time. I appreciate being treated like an intelligent adult, but at the same time, I try to avoid offending people by appearing highfalutin. Even using a term like "highfalutin" can be seen by some as pretentious behavior. H.L. Mencken, that master American wordsmith, discussed the origins of "highfalutin" (an 1848 political speech) and "non-committal" (an 1841 Senate debate) in his classic, "The American Language," and concluded "[b]oth are useful words; it is impossible, not employing them, to convey the ideas behind them without circumlocution."

Fortunately, when it comes to this column, "Circumlocution R Us." The great word history site, **www.Word-Detective.com**

looked at "highfalutin," which it defines as "pompous, arrogant, haughty, pretentious" and "excessively ornate or bombastic, especially in speech." They found two possible but unproven origins, the weakest of which is that it comes from "the airy, delicate speech tones of hoity-toity rich folks." There's no evidence backing that one, but the other's more plausible. It suggests that "highfalutin" comes from "high-flown," meaning "exaggerated or elevated," since "high-flown" has been in use since the mid-1600s.

Highfalutin folks may not care about how they appear, but nobody wants to be thought a dogberry, yet we all know a few. A dogberry is "a pompous, incompetent, and self-important official," the term deriving from a character with that name in Shakespeare's "Much Ado About Nothing." There's much to be said for being precise and informative in interpersonal communications. Matthew Inman's respected, and somewhat raucous, online comic strip, **TheOatmeal.com**, is a surprisingly strong bastion of good grammar, providing humorous examples to help fix the concepts in his readers' minds.

For instance, "Mr. Jenkins often likes to throw spiders at children" is Inman's example for illustrating the difference between "who" and "whom." "Mr. Jenkins" is the sentence's subject, or "who," since he's doing something, and the children having something done to them, are the object, or "whom." However, Inman admits that "'whom' offers no real utility in our language. It does not convey an idea more clearly or effectively than by simply using 'who'... But 'whom' is not about utility or even pedantry... When you use 'whom,' it instantly makes whatever you just said sound distinguished and classy, even if you said something terrible...if you really want to use 'whom' but still can't seem to get the rules straight, try looking for a pronoun such as "you,' 'he,' 'she,' 'they,' 'we" that precedes a verb in the latter half of your sentence." "With who shall I shave my back hair?" for example, can be properly rephrased "With whom."

TheOatmeal boosts the useful semicolon, saying it's helpful

"when you want to form a bond between two statements, typically when they are related or to contrast with one another." Periods — as in "." — date from long ago when everything was read aloud. Then commas indicated to readers a brief pause, and periods showed places to breathe. Semicolons eliminate the pause between two statements using words such as "and," "but," and "nor." Two independent but related clauses, like Inman's "I gnaw on car tires," and "It strengthens my jaws for bear combat" can be joined with semicolons. But "I fought the bear and won" and Also, I never kiss plague rats on the mouth" require a period between them.

Those wary of highfalutiness should beware of abstract nouns; these are nouns that denote ideas, qualities, or states instead of concrete objects. As examples of abstract nouns, the Lexicon of Linguistics gives "democracy" and "wisdom," and it lists "apple" and "water" as concrete nouns. Some modern pundits lamentably enjoy making concrete nouns abstract by adding suffixes like "-cy," -ty," "-ity," "and especially "-ness," creating linguistic monsters like "truthiness" and "hunky-doryness." But that's been going on a long time. Chaucer liked the term "heavity," the opposite of "levity." "Outrageousty" stopped being used in the 1400s, along with "debonairity."

Librarians are often considered to be prone to hoity-toityness, and some may be guilty. But your public librarians aren't afflicted with rigorosity or seriosity. In fact, they're brimming with helpful graciosity.

Dogs, Dr. Seuss, and the Moral Molecule

M ost of my life's been spent in the pleasurable company of dogs, and, like Mark Twain, I believe "The dog is a gentleman; I hope to go to his heaven, not man's." This flies in the face of early and prolonged encounters with P.D. Eastman's "Go, Dog, Go!," one of the famous Beginner Books series co-founded by Dr. Seuss at Random House.

Beginner Books' first title was Seuss' immortal "The Cat in the Hat" of 1957, which he wrote and illustrated to prove that making entertaining reading primers was possible. Working with a 200-word vocabulary, Seuss said he grew so frustrated that he decided to build the story on the first two words that rhymed: "cat" and "hat." An immediate hit, it sold a million copies in three years. "It is the book I am proudest of," Seuss said in 1983, "because it had something to do with the death of the Dick and Jane grammars."

In 1958 there were only four Beginner Book titles, but they earned a million dollars annually and Random House became the leading American children's book publisher. Seuss, whose real name was Ted Geisel, wrote and illustrated some of these books, like "Green Eggs and Ham" and "Hop on Pop," and, using pennames such as Theo LeSieg and Rosetta Stone, also collaborated with other illustrators, like P.D. Eastman. Eastman wrote and illustrated "Go, Dog, Go!" in 1961 when I was nine and beyond primers. However, my mother published my brother in 1961, and I wound up reading Eastman's classic dog book to him a jillion times. Like all the other Beginner Books authors, Eastman utilized simple words and drawings to introduce to children difficult concepts, like colors and relative positions in "Go, Dogs." Repetition helps promote understanding, and kids possess an amazing tolerance for re-reading their favorite books. It can drive their adult readers nuts.

Eastman took pity on his books' grown-up readers by inserting amusing visual diversions here and there. In fact, I still enjoy a rousing, read-aloud rendition of "Go, Dogs, Go!," even after countless bouts of "Go, Dog" with each of my four kiddos,

Yes, I love dogs, and they love me according to an article by Paul Zak in **TheAtlantic.com**. Zak's a researcher at Claremont University and author of "The Moral Molecule" which describes his team's study of oxytocin. His team has "done dozens of studies showing that the brain produces the chemical oxytocin when someone treats us with kindness…it motivates us to treat others with care and compassion." Their studies show that "when humans engage in social activities with each other, oxytocin level typically increase between 10 percent and 50 percent." A stranger shaking your hand might induce a 10 percent rise in your oxytocin, but if they're also attractive it might hit 50. A hug from your daughter can bring on a 100 percent spike, and really huge jumps occur during love-making.

Zak's team studied oxytocin in humans interacting with animals and found "dogs reduced stress hormones better than cats (no surprise there!)." Apparently, the more dogs in your past life is a predictor of increased levels of oxytocin, and more cats predicts reduced oxytocin. Moreover, last year a Massachusetts man filed an Americans with Disabilities Act suit against his public library for having a cat live there and inflicting its dander on allergy suffering patrons.

The American Lung Foundation reports that twice as many people are allergic to cats, especially female felines, compared to dogs. The Asthma and Allergy Foundation notes that cat dander is particularly sticky and can trigger severe attacks in 20 to 30 percent of asthma sufferers. The recommended treatment for dander is to remove the animal's favorite furniture, and all carpeting, and scrub all walls and woodwork. Or you could simply forego living with cats.

After an uproar by cat-lovers, and after agreeing to not allow any more cats, the ADA lawsuit against the Massachusetts library was dropped. But even that compromise is a mistake in my estimation. Your right to utilize your public library is constitutionally protected by federal court ruling from the late 1990s, and cats shouldn't impede that.

Library dogs are another matter. Therapeutic reading with dogs has been shown to help many children. After all, like Andy Rooney noted, "The average dog is a nicer person than the average person."

Grammar Nazis, Word Power, and Shakespeare's Library

....

Truly, I'm no grammar Nazi. I've known real ones — some of my best friends are grammatical storm troopers — but I know that some slang evolves into perfectly good vocabulary fodder. English's embracing flexibility is what makes it so fresh and vibrant, yet my soul writhes when our language is needlessly mutilated by cumbersomely-formed terms. Take the new verb "efforting," for example. "Effort," defined by Macmillan Dictionary as "an attempt to do something that is difficult," is a widely-recognized noun, but "efforting," which means "trying," is only defined in one of the 1,061 dictionaries in the **OneLook.com** database. That singularity is the user-written **UrbanDictionary.com** which defines itself as a "place formerly used to find out about slang, and now a place that teens with no life use as a burn book to whine about celebrities, their friends, etc., let out their sexual frustrations, show off their racist/sexist/homophobic/anti-(insert religion here) opinions, troll, and babble about things they know nothing about."

It's certainly not the American Heritage, Oxford English, or even Webster's Collegiate Dictionaries, where you won't find "efforting" but will see "attempt," "endeavor," "try," "strive," "venture," "work at," among others. "Efforting's" awkwardness exacerbates matters. It's not like so many graceful English expressions that have dropped by time's wayside, like in the Victorian sentence, "Those skilamalink bludgers are all gigglemugged what with their mafficking nanty-narking and smothering a parrot or two." It translates as "Those shady criminals are constantly smiling thanks to their boisterous fun at the pub following their imbibing the hallucinatory beverage absinthe."

"The power of words is immense," as the 19th century French journalist Emile de Girardin pointed out. "A well-chosen word has often sufficed to stop a flying army, to change defeat into victory, and to save an empire." Nobody's combined words as well as Shakespeare. His inventions include such house-hold words and phrases as "house-hold words," "foregone conclusion," "fool's paradise," "a sorry sight," "dead as a doornail," "a charmed life," "one fell swoop," "fair play," "in a pickle," "exceedingly well read," and well over a hundred more.

So where did Shakespeare pick up his wide vocabulary, not to mention his grasp of French, Italian, and Latin? Few people have been so thoroughly researched, and the sources of most of Shakespeare's plays have been determined. The 1587 edition of "Holingshed's Chronicles," for instance, was a comprehensive history of Britain, and parts of it closely correspond to the events in "Macbeth," "King Lear," and most of Shakespeare's history plays. He also had a friend's library to draw upon for new storylines and words.

London had no public libraries then, but Richard Field, a boyhood pal from Stratford, was an apprentice to a leading London printer. Printers were also publishers and booksellers, and one of Field's masters was a French refugee named Vautrollier. Field was accepted into the printer's guild days before Vautrollier died, whereupon he married Vautrollier's widow and, at age 26, took over the business, including the shop's extensive bookstock. Field went on to publish a slew of books Shakespeare would utilize, including French and Latin word books, that enabled the self-starting Bard the means to work his verbal magic.

Two rare book dealers believe they've bought Shakespeare's own polyglot dictionary on eBay for $4,300 and want to sell it for a bit more. A recent New Yorker article by Adam Gopnik says the sixteenth century book, "a second edition of John Baret's 'Alvearie' (a variant of 'apiary'), is not exactly a dictionary in the modern sense...a word appears in English and its equivalents are usually offered in French and Latin and Greek, often with a proverbial expression or citation from a classical author. It is a compendium of allusions." Perfect for a word-lover like the Bard, and this one might include his margin notes.

"What's sure," Gopnik adds, "is that Shakespeare was, like many other self-taught people, a bookish guy...he got himself educated in modern languages and literature by buying or borrowing books, and burrowing inside them." Today he'd utilize his public library, which provides the resources for everyone to educate, entertain, enlighten, and express themselves. And if you're among the minority who don't, then, as Shakespeare put it, "more fool you."

Creative Forgetting, Word Bubbles, and Curious Minds

Certain parts of the English vocabulary seem geographically predisposed. For example, to my ear, "metropolitan," "youse," and "commuter train" smack of East Coast urban life, though pertaining to other regions as well. "Sashay," on the other hand, evokes a drowsy summer day in the South, as do "mosey" and "saunter." I'm a child of the South and was chagrined recently to have to plead ignorance when asked to distinguish between "sashay," "mosey," and "saunter." Fortunately, there's no shame in ignorance if you do something about it. I did and now know "sashay" is from the French "chasse" ballet movement, "saunter" is "probably from the Middle English 'santren,' meaning 'to muse,'" but "mosey" is more local, deriving from "vamos," Mexican Spanish for "we go."

Moreover, sashayers "strut or move in a showy manner," while saunterers "stroll at a leisurely pace" and moseyers "stroll in no particular hurry." And what about their verbal cousins? Amblers take "a leisurely, pleasurable walk," rambler's tend to "go on and on," and gallivanters "meander from one place to another in search of fun." Knowing the fine distinctions between similar terms enables writers to paint effective word-pictures that similarly-skilled readers can appreciate. But how does one acquire those more esoteric words in the first place?

A 2011 study by University of Pennsylvania professors reported

13

in Science Daily support other recent research disproving "associative learning," the long-held belief "that children learn their first
words through a series of associations; they associate words they
hear with multiple possible referents in their immediate environment. Over time, children can track both the words and elements of
the environments they correspond to, eventually narrowing down
what common element the word must be referring to."

That appears plausible, especially in a laboratory setting, but
the article quotes the lead Penn researcher, Lila Gleitman, saying
"It turns out it's probably impossible" because in the real world,
immediate environments "contain essentially an infinite number of
meaning options." There are simply too many possibilities to sort
through for efficient learning and communication to take place.
Instead, the UPenn research showed that children learned words
"in a 'eureka' moment" instead of through simple rote repetition
used in associative learning.

The research also studied how we manage to quickly forget
incorrect word associations. "All those memories go away, Gleitman
said. "And that's great! It's the failure of memory that's rescuing
you from remaining wrong all your life." As the recently-deceased
Gabriel Garcia Marquez pointed out, "The heart's memory elimi-
nates the bad and magnifies the good."

A paper published this month in Science describes studies into
why we can't recall memories from early childhood. "The brain
makes new cells throughout life — a process called neurogenesis —
but young people produce new neurons at a much higher rate. And
this process is particularly active in the hippocampus, which deals
with memories and learning...the extremely high rate of neurogenesis seen in very young children can actually increase forgetfulness."

Based upon that hypothesis, it appears I've been undergoing
amazing levels of neurogenesis. Whatever the cause, my shaky
memory's been a lifelong complaint, dooming my attempts to learn
foreign languages, remember birthdays, and all the ingredients to
that great artichoke dip.

It extends to my vocabulary as well, especially "the bubble vocabulary," as described in a **Slate.com** article by Seth Stevenson titled "Shibboleth, Causitry, Recondite." Stevenson defines "bubble vocabulary" as "the words you almost know, sometimes use, but are secretly unsure of." Such words are legion for many experienced readers. We encounter words and believe we've figured out their rough meanings within the context of the surrounding passage, but aren't certain. Sample words include "execrable," "folderol," "and prima facie." The article includes an 18-word test drawn from Slate staffers' bubble vocabularies that you can test your vocabulary against.

Exercising the mind is critical for keeping it sharp, and, being chock-full of mental stimulation, the public library makes a marvelous gym. The important thing is staying curious about the world and doing something about it. "Anyone who stops learning is old, whether at 2 or 80," as Moshe Arens said. "Anyone who keeps learning stays young. The greatest thing in life is to keep your mind young."

Brewer's Dictionary, Jenkin's Ear, and How Far Athletes Run

B rewer's Dictionary of Phrase and Fable, that thick collection of concise explanations and curiosities is perfect for lazy, rainy June afternoons. The wanderings of Turkey's fabled Meander River don't compare to those in Brewer's. For example, it's difficult to look up "groat," "the name given to all thick silver coins, from Middle Dutch 'groot,'" which meant "thick," without also encountering "grog, "the name given to the British seaman's twice-daily drink composed of a half-pint of neat spirits mixed with a pint of water. No one called it grog early on, but they started doing so in 1740 when Admiral Edward Vernon cut the liquor in half.

A Member of Parliament when Captain Robert Jenkin's ear was cut off by the Spanish Coast Guard in 1731, Vernon quickly became Jenkin's most vocal advocate. The situation with Spain festered until 1739, when Britain declared war and Admiral Vernon was named commander of the West Indies fleet. According to **MilitaryHistory. About.Com**, "the following year saw Vernon order that the daily rum ration provided to the sailors be watered down to three parts water and one part rum in an effort to reduce drunkenness. To offset the often brackish taste of the water, lemon or lime juice was added to the mixture. As Vernon was known as 'Old Grog' for his habit of wearing grogham coats, the new drink became known as grog."

"Grogham," Brewer's tells us, is "a coarse fabric made from silk and mohair or silk and wool, stiffened with gum." The phrase "old fashioned" is what I originally looked for in Brewer's, and Old Grog was an old-fashioned guy, at least sartorially. Yet he was quite innovative, for besides the accidental side-benefit that including lime juice prevented scurvy, the lower general inebriation among the crew caused a marked decline in other work-related injuries.

The World Cup of soccer is underway, and that's a big deal to those who understand the sport and appreciate its demanding nature. **Gizmodo.com** ran a "How Far Do You Run" article stating that basketball players top out at 2.72 miles per game, baseball outfielders hitting four home runs in a game will run less than a half-mile, and football receivers and defensive backs hit a maximum of 1.25 miles per game. In fact, the Wall Street Journal found that football players move only eleven of the sixty-minutes in a game.

In soccer "it's not uncommon for a player to average seven miles a game… SportVU has tracked players running as much as 9.5 miles in a game." I played men's soccer year-round for sixteen years and, after a few kicked legs and run-ins with water-logged leather balls, I learned to appreciate innovations like shin-guards and synthetic balls. But I get quite curmudgeonly when it comes to sportsmanship and fair play. A recent New York Times article focused on how the US men's soccer team is known for not faking injuries or other shenanigans like most other international soccer players. Sadly that was described by the author as a fault instead of a virtue.

Once I read that Zsa Zsa Gabor claimed to be "very old-fashioned," while Barbara Bush said she's "a little old-fashioned," and Cher stated, "I'm not old-fashioned." Like the Admiral, I land close to Barbara on the Gabor-Cher continuum. On one hand, I've witnessed a lot of changes in libraries over three decades of running them, but I still find the traditional ideals represented by our public libraries to be deeply moving and relevant in today's world.

The value of old-fashioned things lies in their track record. Most American cities have had public libraries for more than a century that still enjoy enormous popular support. Here in our borough, for instance, nearly six out of ten residents — men, women, and children — possess library cards that they've used within the last two years, and hundreds use the library without borrower cards every week. For five thousand years people have expected their libraries to gather information, organize and protect it, and disseminate it to the intended audience. Libraries may utilize computers and digital information to accomplish these missions, but the underlying, old-fashioned purposes are unchanged.

How entrenched is the library in the American way of life? Imagine life without it. "Eden is that old-fashioned house we dwell in every day," as Emily Dickinson put it, "Without suspecting our abode, until we drive away."

OMG!, Recency, and Soccer

....

The old Scottish poet Allan Cunningham once wrote about a time "when looks were fond and words were few." That was when etymology, "the study of the origins and development of words," wasn't needed. Often confused with entomology, the study of insects, etymology tracks how words and their meanings have morphed over time. Here in the Information Age words increasingly abound, and we need all the etymology we can get. Consider the debate over "soccer" and "football." Many British sports fans take umbrage over Americans calling their sport "soccer," since the game was originally organized in England in 1863 as the Football Association.

Early American-style football was much like England's, but it evolved into a sport "that mostly involves people doing things to the ball with their hands," as noted in a recent NY Times article by Sarah Lyall titled "Up in Arms Over 'Soccer.'" "Association football" provided rules that civilized the extremely violent ancient game that sprang up around the world in many civilizations, beginning with the ancient Chinese and Egyptians. Lyall described how a fad arose among college students in Victorian England "to add the infantilizing 'er' diminutive to random words," and, according to the Online Etymology Dictionary, they also enjoyed shortening names. So they abbreviated "Assoc.," the abbreviation of "Association," into "Soc," which was "an unusual method of [word] formation, but those who did it perhaps shied away from making a name out of the first three letters of 'Assoc.'"

"Discussing this exciting new sport in 1905 and 1906," Lyall wrote, "the New York Times seized on 'soccer' as useful shorthand, particularly in space-challenging headlines. But only sometimes. Other times it spelled it 'socker.'" The English spelling was "socca" in 1889, "socker" in 1891, and "soccer" in 1895. "The problem came in the 1970s and '80s," Lyall cites Stefan Szymanski, a University of Michigan sports management professor saying. "As the sport became more of a force in the United States…[t]hat threatened people, and the English particularly…and caused them to go on violent rants on the topic of Americans' obnoxious and perverse tendency to do things differently from everyone else."

This illustrates the "recency illusion," which linguist Arnold Zwicky defines as "the belief that things you have noticed only recently are in fact recent." It's discussed in an article in **TheGuardian.com** by David Shariatmandari titled "11 Words That Are Much Older Than You Think." He describes a popular "prejudice about language: that it's gradually deteriorating" and "is part of a broader cognitive bias that leads us to extrapolate from our own experience to make theories about the world… [t]hankfully, there's a big chunk of actual data on the history of English to check our assumptions against: it's called literature."

Zwicky's found a bunch of surprises by comparing modern lingo to written English. A modern hipster might say "I asked that babe to hang out in my crib, but she said 'OMG! Not!' So I unfriended her." The Oxford English Dictionary states that "babe," as in "She's some babe," appeared in the American Dialect Society's journal in 1915. Shakespeare had King Henry the IV ask, "Why rather, sleep, liest thou in smokey cribs, Upon uneasy pallets stretching thee… Than in the perfumed chambers of the great?" "OMG," meaning "Oh, my God," was used in a 1917 letter to Winston Churchill from his predecessor as First Sea Lord.

George Eliot's "Mill on the Floss" includes the line "She would make a sweet, strange, troublesome, adorable wife to some man or other...but he would never have chosen her himself. Did she feel as he did? He hoped she did — not." And back in 1659 the English historian Thomas Fuller wrote an acquaintance, "I Hope, Sir, that we are not mutually Un-friended by this Difference witch hath happened betwixt us."

"All words are pegs to hang ideas on," as Henry Beecher Ward wrote, and their usefulness to humankind is obvious. Civilization requires the ability to communicate abstract concepts, and words, spoken, written, or thought, facilitate that process. That's why libraries, where our printed words and ideas are preserved for the 500-year life expectancy of acid-free paper, remain so popular with the thinking public.

Hyphenites, Assonance, and Monkeyshines

....

L ast week brought a new appreciation for animal-oriented names, especially daddy long-leg spiders, carpenter ants, and the expression "monkeyshines." But first, let's consider the hyphen. Though not a "hyphenite," which, according to **UrbanDictionary. com** is a newly-minted word for "a type of racist" who employs terms such as "Mexican-American" instead of saying "American." I do admire grammatical hyphens, as defined by the Macmillan Dictionary: "the short line (-) used for joining two written words or parts of words, or for dividing a word at the end of a line of writing." Since these columns are limited to 700 words, humble hyphens have occasionally helped me reach that demarcation.

It's an old word, coming from the Greek "huphen," meaning "a sign indicating a compound word or two words which are to be read as one." Hyphenation was recently discussed at the online Daily Writing Tips website, particularly "a trend towards having the prefixes and suffixes separate from the modified noun instead of being attached or hyphenated," like "non negotiable" and "post surgery." A discussion of the prefixes "non-" and "post-" and the suffix "-wise" ensued, but there were two main upshots. First, American dictionaries tend to make one word out of two words that the British dictionaries usually hyphenate, and second, "hyphenation is not an exact science," which is good news for this rabid hyphenator.

A surprising University of California, Riverside report began "Daddy-Longlegs are one of the most poisonous spiders, but their

22

fangs are too short to bite humans." They go on to say that's a popular myth, and the insect known as daddy-longlegs, daddy long-legs, or daddy longlegs, according to your hyphenating inclinations, is instead a benign scavenger. Daddy-longlegs and daddy-longlegs spiders are entirely different creatures. The first are of the Opiliones Order not spiders, and have two eyes versus the eight eyes found on the equally spindley-legged spiders that resemble them.

There are some "badly broken words," according to an article by James Harbeck on **TheWeek.com** website. He described how words can be formed from several bits of words over time, only to evolve into shortened words that don't match the original parts. "Helicopter," for example, didn't come from "helio" and "copter," but from the Greek "helicos," or "spiral," and "pteron," or "wing." "Info" is derived from "information," which comes from combining "in," "form," and "ation." "To inform someone is to shape their knowledge — to put it 'in form.' Or, for the short version, "info."

Last week the website **A.Word.A.Day** featured "words that sound dirty, but aren't." "Assonance," for instance, means "The use of words with same or similar vowel sounds but with different end consonants," as in "the o sounds in Wordsworth's 'A hot of golden daffodils." "Inspissate," on the other hand, means "to thicken or condense," and "formicate" is defined as "to crawl with ants" with "formica" being Latin for "ant." This caught my attention, for I'd just perused the public library's copy of "Carpenter Ants of the

United States and Canada" by Laurel Hansen, since our woodland home is being visited by more of these guys than usual. Despite my antipathy for them, it was fascinating to learn how they spray formic acid for defense and have topochemical sensing that allows them to use scent molecules to denote height and other dimensions

"Monkeyshines," on the other hand, sounds innocent but isn't. I came across a 2007 article from **GrammarPhobia.com** that mentioned the word's roots. "It first appeared in 1828 as 'munky shines' in a song by Thomas 'Daddy' Rice, a popular white comedian who performed in blackface. In the song 'Jump Jim Crow,' Rice sings and dances as an old plantation slave: 'I cut so many munky shines, I dance de gallopande'...a 19th century dance. The song also gave us the term 'Jim Crow' for segregation."

I love dancing with words and learning their origins and distinctions, even when they're disturbing. "When I use a word," Humpty Dumpty said in a rather scornful tone, "it means just what I choose it to mean — neither more nor less." "The question is," said Alice, "whether you can make words mean so many different things." "The question is, said Humpty Dumpty, "which is to be master — that's all."

Duck Bill Hickock, the Influential Rich, and Public Libraries

The first wild west shootout occurred 99 years ago last week when the gambler Bill Hickok and cowboy David Tutt squared off over women, money, and a pocket watch. It seems that Bill, a former scout for the Union army, might have impregnated Confederate veteran Tutt's sister, while Tutt was flirting with Hickok's main squeeze. Things came to a head when Hickok refused to play cards with Tutt, who in turn bankrolled some friends to play in his stead. They lost $200 of Tutt's money, and he snatched Hickok's pocket watch, claiming Hickok owed him money. Surrounded by Tutt's buddies, Hickok didn't argue but warned him not to wear it in public. They met in the town square the next day, walked 75 paces apart, and simultaneously pulled their handguns and fired. Tutt fired first but missed, while the more deliberate Hickok plugged his adversary through the heart.

The best source on his topic is Bill O'Neal's "The Encyclopedia of Western Gunfighters," where you'll learn that Hickok's first deadly dustup happened four years earlier in 1861. He was working as a lowly stagecoach attendant and messing around with the paramour of a local rancher named McCanles, who enjoyed "calling Hickok 'Duck Bill,' a slur upon his facial features, and 'hermaphrodite,' a slur upon certain other of his features." It wasn't the sort of gunfight featured in countless westerns. McCanles called him out, but Hickok refused to leave the stage station. When McCanles entered the building, he "was promptly shot to death by Hickok," who was hiding behind a curtain.

Most of the 587 gunfights listed in the book are similarly ignoble, but all "involved men who proved themselves professionals." The majority of the shootouts took place in Texas, "the most violent western area, and they were most common in the 1870s and early 1880s," with the last coming when lawman Bill Tilghman was gunned down in 1924. Many gunfighters sported nicknames based on physical characteristics (Flat Nose Curry and Cockeyed Frank Loving), personality traits (Happy Jack Morco and Mysterious Dave Mather), and "occupational tendencies" (Doc Holliday and Dynamite Dick Clifton).

It took brave men to wrangle with these desperadoes, and while some found fame, like Bat Masterson and Pat Garrett, most didn't get rich doing it, which brings up a recent study from Duke University that asked 1,519 American participants what they'd do for $1 million. On the positive side, seven in eight said they wouldn't kick a friendly dog in the head, but twenty percent said they would sign a statement saying "I hereby sell my soul, after my death, to whoever has this piece of paper," and all but 6 percent said they'd do it for less than $1 million, and 3 percent said they'd do it for free.

Really rich people are oblivious to such temptations. A "Perspectives in Politics" article by Martin Gilens analyzed 1,779 governmental policy outcomes over 20 years and concluded that "economic elites and organized groups representing business interests have substantial independent impacts on U.S. government policy, while mass-based interest groups and average citizens have little or no independent influence." The Washington Post article on this study adds that "the collective preferences of ordinary citizens had only a negligible estimated impact on policy outcomes, while the collective preferences of 'economic elites' (citizens at the 90th percentile of the income distribution) were 15 times as important."

It's no wonder so many Americans don't vote or get involved in civic concerns. Still, it's interesting to compare that sad fact to how many of our fellow citizens utilize their public libraries to obtain important information, handle personal business, boost their educational pursuits, and otherwise improve their lives. Last December the Pew Research Center reported that about half of all Americans used their public libraries the previous year.

Modern public libraries aggregate information affordably, and help their users navigate the plethora of information swamping our modern society. It's not like that in most countries. At your American public library you can say, like Butch Cassidy, "I have a vision, and the rest of the world wears bifocals."

Careful Words, Commas, and CIA Style

....

Buddha once said, "Whatever words we utter should be chosen with care, for people will hear them and be influenced by them for good or ill." He was seconded by Raymond Chandler's "The High Window," in which hard-boiled detective Philip Marlowe encountered a "long-limbed, languorous type of showgirl blond." "From thirty feet away she looked like a lot of class," Marlowe thought, but that was dispelled when she opened her mouth and said "don't" instead of "doesn't" improperly along with other grammatical misstatements. "Where's your refinement?" Marlow wondered.

Decent grammar's important everywhere, because everyone's constantly judged by those they attempt to communicate with. Perusing my copy of "The Meaning of Tingo and Other Extraordinary Words From Around the World," for example, I learned that "speaking a language incorrectly and brokenly" in Turkey is called "catra patra," and similar disapprobation exists in all languages.

Even tiny grammatical flaws can mushroom into serious ramifications. Take the false period in the original Declaration of Independence. Last summer the NY Times reported that a researcher is questioning "a period that appears right after the phrase 'life, liberty, and the pursuit of happiness,' but almost certainly not... on the badly faded parchment original." That sentence continues "instituted among men, deriving their power from the consent of the governed." The period isn't in Jefferson's original rough draft or the broadside Congress had printed. Without it "the importance of government as a tool" in protecting individual rights is emphasized.

Other small grammatical slips can loom large, like a missing comma turning "Let's eat, grandma!" into the disturbing "Let's eat grandma!" And during the funeral ceremonies for Nelson Mandela last December the Washington Times reported on a Britain's Sky News headline that read, "World leaders at Mandela tribute, Obama-Castro handshake and same-sex marriage date set." "The prospect of a wedding between the two world leaders got the Twitterverse tweeting. 'This is why the Oxford comma exists!' said Carole Blake, a literary agent in London. The Oxford comma is that extra punctuation mark before the word 'and' that the British use and Americans usually don't."

Count me in among the many American proponents of the Oxford, or 'serial,' comma. Other advocates on this side of the Atlantic include the U.S. Government Printing Office, the Chicago Manual of Style, the CIA, and the redoubtable "Elements of Style," by William Strunk, Jr, and E.B. White. "Strunk and White," as "Elements of Style" is popularly known, is the quintessential book on the art of skillful writing. When my well-read and spoken eldest child recently challenged her family and acquaintances to come up with a "ten-books-that-changed-your-life" list, you better believe "Strunk and White" was on mine.

My first copy was given to me by my boss at the State Department after he'd read a preliminary draft of my first report. Strunk and White's wisdom was revelatory, and quite literally changed my life. A comma's a small price to avoid ambiguity, so when Strunk and White state "In a series of three or more terms with a single conjunction, use a comma after each term," as in "red, white, and blue," instead of "red, white and blue," that's good enough for me.

Strunk and White's staunch recommendations pale next to the Central Intelligence Agency's "Style Manual & Writers Guide for Intelligence Publications." "The CIA's ruthless style manual," as the American Press Institute terms it, was made public last July through a Freedom of Information Act request from the legal non-profit National Security Counselors and the API was quick to note that the document cites its heavy reliance on "Elements of Style." The API added that "the CIA is a prescriptivist scold, a believer in the serial comma, and a champion of 'crisp and pungent' language 'devoid of jargon.'"

Being such a Strunk and White fanboy, many CIA style recommendations seem fine, like "omit the extraneous, no matter how brilliant it may seem or even be," and "Keep sentences and paragraphs short, and vary the structure of both." However, the CIA's darker side's present as well. The manual makes special distinctions between similar but confusing terms, like "disinformation" ("deliberate planting of false reports") and "misinformation" ("equates in meaning but does not carry the same devious connotation"), and "tortuous" ("twisting, devious, highly complex") and "torturous" ("causing torture, cruelly painful").

As Mark Twain pointed out, "A man's character may be learned from the adjectives which he habitually uses in conversation."

Demonyms, Pedants, and Reading for Fun

....

"**G**enerous" and "thoughtful" were labels that came to mind when I received a book in the mail titled "Labels for Locals: What to Call People from Abilene to Zimbabwe" and read the enclosed card from author Paul Dickson that mentioned his enjoying my columns and making a gift to our library of his informative book.

Dickson's book of "demonyms," or "a name for a resident of a particular locality," is "meant to be used by those who want to find the proper form — or forms — of address or reference for people in a particular locale." Having grown up in Abilene, Texas, I was pleased to see he got "Abilenian" right, but the "Alaskan" entry was more interesting. "[T]here is some resistance to its use as an adjective," Dickson noted. He cites the respected Russell Tabbert, author of "Dictionary of Alaskan English": "I have heard from some Alaskan journalists and read in some of their style sheets the claim that 'Alaskan' should be used only as a noun referring to a person and should never be used as an adjective. However," Tabbert added, "this rule certainly doesn't fit Alaskan usage, including much journalistic usage."

The label "pedantic," or "giving too much importance to details and formal rules, especially of grammar," is popping up more frequently, following a trend towards picking nits generally, especially online. A number of hoary English grammar rules sprang from well-intentioned Victorian classists who wanted to impose

the rigid regularity of Latin upon our inconsistent English. Many
of these rules, like "no dangling participles," have been abandoned
by popular usage. Some were overly-contrived from the get-go.
As Debra Crosby, my favorite online grammarian, recently posted,
"I before e, except when you run a feisty heist on a weird beige
foreign neighbor."

The Internet abounds with incorrect misspellings and flawed
grammar, which invariably drives some well-lettered friends to
distraction and occasions them to post corrections online. Is this
pedantry, or is it justifiable raging against the darkness of miscom-
munication? And how to take well-meaning online articles like
"Five Thinking Strategies of Good Readers," drawn from an excerpt
of Brenda Smith's "Breaking Through to College Reading"?

Smith's strategies include "Form Images," "Draw Comparisons,"
and "Check Understanding." "For good readers," Smith writes,
"the words and the ideas on the page trigger mental images that
relate directly or indirectly to the material. Images are like movies
in your head." She suggests comparing what you're reading to your
existing knowledge, and keeping "an internal summary or synthesis
of the information as it is presented and how it relates to the overall
message" while supervising your own comprehension." The other
strategies were "Make educated guesses" and "Do not accept gaps
in your reading comprehension."

That's easier said than done, especially while reading, and imagine low-level readers trying to follow that advice. My recommended
strategy for reading promotion is: "Make It Fun." Reading's difficult, but we crave entertainment, and reading's far easier when it's
also thrilling, hilarious, informative, or intriguing, for our brains
are wired to "Delight in the Unexpected." That's the subtitle of
a 1963 Atlantic Magazine article by Walt Kelly, creator of the
Pogo comic strip. Kelly wrote that "Inserting bounces into already
formed speech, you get something like 'horribobble.' There is no
deep meaning behind the device... The Pogo speech pattern is full
of noises signifying nothing more than the grunts of a determined

grandfather eating corn." Humorists know that humans find amusing verbal discombobulates engaging.

Kelly suggested not getting bogged down in rules. To get kids reading, "It is not important to communicate exact shades of meaning, but it is necessary to get across a sense of fun." The fun goes out of reading for many boys around third and fourth grades, so the locally-grown Fairbanks Guys Read program has won awards by showing those very boys how much fun books can be by featuring books that are "boy-friendly" in content and accessible to low-level readers while entertaining good readers.

While the boys read silly books for the sheer fun of it, they're honing vocabulary, comprehension, and other skills that will carry over into more serious reading. "Reader" is a pretty good label to aspire for, and as Star Trek's George Takei noted, "A child who reads will be an adult who thinks."

Life-Long Learning, Degorging, and Zeugmas

....

Our local Osher Lifelong Learning Institute is a joy. Learning for its own sake's a rich experience, and skipping class and improving upon the teacher's insights with impunity are marvelous bonuses. Those enrolled in OLLI's Mastering Wine 101 course are particularly diligent scholars, and instructor Kathy Lavelle, a certified wine professional, receives rapt attention and little sass from her enthralled class. It's a jolly gathering anyway, but some of the oenological vocabulary introduced recently inspired added mirth. "Degorging" engendered wild mental imagery until Kathy explained that this is a vintner's process of removing sediment from aging champagne by chilling the upturned bottles until the sediment congeals. Internal pressure shoots it out of the bottle when the cap's removed, and the bottle's then topped up with more wine and re-corked.

Also amusing were the Old Testament names of the enormous bottles favored by collectors of rare Bordeaux wines, like the 16-bottle Balthazars and 20-bottle Nebuchadnezzars. I was thrown by the mention of "surly wines." Too many wines in my usual price range qualified as "surly." However, later consultation with Noel Wien Library's copy of the Oxford Companion to Wine revealed that the reference was to "sur lie" wines. "Lees" is Old English for the French "lies," meaning sedimentary dregs. So "sur lie" means "upon the lees" and describes wine that's had the skins and other natural detritus left in the wine for a while for flavoring.

Confusing words were featured in a contest sponsored recently by **A.Word.A.Day.** Subscribers to the free service submitted entries in several categories, including zeugmas, antimetaboles, and synecdoches. Bob's Poetic Byway online site defines "zeugma" as "a figure of speech in which a single word, usually a verb or adjective, is used in the same grammatical and semantic relationship with two or more other words." The contest's winning zeugma, for instance, was, "He checked out the book and the librarian." "Antimetaboles" repeat words or ideas in reverse order. "The rat race creates a race of rats" is a sample entry. The "synecdoche" is a "figure of speech in which a part stands for the whole or vice versa," as in "She's the head librarian."

Words can also be hurtful, sometimes intentionally so, as the awful political season exemplified. An example is pundit George Will's assertion that President Obama's heavy use of personal pronouns in his speeches reveals a pervasive, unbalanced narcissism. A University of Pennsylvania analysis revealed that, by this measure, Obama is the third least narcissistic of the fourteen men who've held that office since 1935, trailing only Hoover and FDR.

If you want true narcissism find an Internet troll, defined by the American Heritage Dictionary as "a person who posts inflammatory or otherwise unwanted material on an electronic forum, especially anonymously." Their best-known tactic is to post an online comment that's so outrageous it gets responses from indignant readers. "A New Study Shows That Internet Trolls Really Are Just Terrible People," a Canadian study cited in **PsychologyToday.com**, described the "Dark Tryad," an especially nefarious combination of personality traits: narcissism, Machiavellianism ("manipulation and exploitation of others," according to Wikipedia), and psychopathy ("antisocial behavior, impulsivity, selfishness, callousness, and remorselessness"). The study found that "Dark Tryad scores were highest among people who said trolling was their favorite Internet activity...it might be said that online trolls are prototypical everyday sadists...the best thing you can do is ignore them."

Thank goodness **MentalFloss.com** published "25 of the Happiest Words in English," by Arika Orkent. It describes how some University of Vermont mathematicians took 10,000 words found in sources like Google Books, the NY Times, Twitter, and music lyrics and had people rate them on a scale from least to most happy. "Laughter" and "terrorist" came in first and last, respectively, but when it came to the others, "it turns out that positivity heaped on positivity becomes, like sugar or a giant clown smile, sickening after a point." The other top words, for example, were "happiness," "love," "happy," "laughed," "laugh," etc. Okrent suggested that some lower-scored words are "anchors of true quiet positivity in a sea of toothy grins," including "interesting" (172), "dinner" (239), and "agree" (947).

"Warmth" would probably score higher in Alaska than 375th. And, as Captain Kangaroo foretold, "please" and "thanks" are always magical.

Feckless Similes and P.G. Wodehouse

The origin of the word "feck" arose following mention of P.G. Wodehouse's skilled use of back-formations in last week's column. A back-formation occurs when a shorter word is made out of a longer one, like when one of Wodehouse's characters "may not be entirely disgruntled, but he was far from gruntled." Having been culpable of occasional fecklessness over the years, I've often wondered how to acquire feck, and what it is. According to the Online Etymology Dictionary, it became popular around 1500 to combine the Scots' "feck," which was a back-formation of "effect," with "less" to make "feckless" and mean "lacking purpose or vitality, careless and irresponsible." The modern usage of feck is "an informal Irish euphemism" for a similar naughty word according to the Dublin Slang Dictionary.

I find novels with obligatory sexual encounters tiresome and divert readers from the storyline. Naughty words won't be found in Wodehouse's ninety-six books, nor in the sixteen plays and twenty-eight musicals he helped write because their high level of amusement made it unnecessary. In an article titled "The Genius of Wodehouse," Roger Kimball, The New Criterion's editor and publisher, quoted writer Hilaire Belloc who commented on fellow-author Wodehouse's authorial ability in 1939: "The end of writing is the production of a certain image and a certain emotion. And the means to that end are the use of words in any particular language; and the complete use of that medium is the choosing of the right words and the putting of them into the right order. It is THIS which Mr. Wodehouse does better, in the English language, than anyone else alive."

"Belloc particularly admired Wodehouse's similes," Kimball noted, "citing as an example his description of Honoria Glossop as 'one of those robust, dynamic girls with the muscles of a welterweight and a laugh like a squadron of cavalry charging over a tin bridge.'" That's a personal favorite, too, but Wodehouse was amazingly prolific, peppering nearly every page with inventively original similes and metaphors.

Other Wodehouseisms include "Some minds are like soup in a poor restaurant — better left unstirred," and "Musical comedy is the Irish stew of drama. Anything may be put into it with the certainty that it will improve the general effect." The first is a simile, "a figure of speech in which two essentially unlike things are compared, often in a phrase introduced by 'like' or 'as'." For another example, Wodehouse wrote about a woman who "looked as if she had been poured into her clothes and had forgotten to say 'when'."

All similes are metaphors, but not all metaphors are similes. Similes are a type of metaphor, which is broadly defined by the American Heritage Dictionary as "a figure of speech in which a word or phrase that ordinarily designates one thing is used to designate another, thus making an implicit comparison, as in Shakespeare's 'All the world's a stage.'"

Similes from Wodehouse's pen include, "A sort of gulpy, gurgly, plobby, squishy, wofflesome sound, like a thousand eager men drinking soup in a foreign restaurant," and "He felt like a man who, chasing rainbows, has had one of them suddenly turn and bite him in the leg." Examples of his metaphors are "Into the face of the young man…there had crept a look of furtive shame, the shifty, hangdog look which announces that an Englishman is about to speak French," and "the supply of the milk of human kindness was short by several gallons." Wodehouse also employed "submerged similes" that don't include the 'like' or 'as' comparatives, as in "She gave me the sort of look she would have given a leper she wasn't fond of."

Books are usually better than movie versions or other adaptations, but Wodehouse is an exception. His stories translate well as audio books, especially those narrated by Jonathan Cecil, and Hugh Laurie and Stephen Fry's BBC adaptations on DVD are hilarious and well-produced, although as Fry has written, "no actors are as good as the actors we each of us carry in our heads." Nonetheless, enormously entertaining Wodehouse CDs, DVDs, and ebooks are at your pubic library, ready to lighten spirits with his gentle, clever comedy, or, as Wodehouse phrased it, "the kindly contemplation of the incongruous." .

Tyrannio the Rapscallion Librarian

....

"Tyrannio" would be a great name for a library director, and, in fact, it was. His real name was Theophrastus, but his disposition was such that a teacher aptly nicknamed him Tyrannio. If you owned a new library full of books looted from Greece and Egypt 2,000 years ago, like Sulla, the general who'd raided Athens in 86 B.C.E., confiscated Aristotle's tattered personal library and took it home to Rome, then Tyrannio, the best librarian in the world, was the guy you'd want to repair and organize it. After taking care of Sulla's books, Tyrannio revamped Cicero's fabulous library, and in his spare time, he accumulated his own 30,000 volume collection.

In today's terms, a comparably-sized library to Tyrannio's would be UAF's Rasmuson Library. Roman librarians administered staffs of literate scribal slaves who copied old and borrowed books to add to their masters' libraries, and Tyrannio usually had his scribes run off extra copies for himself. After his access to Sulla's and Cicero's libraries, Tyrannio had compiled one of the most complete set of Aristotle's works in the world, many of which wouldn't have survived otherwise.

Librarians are often portrayed as meek, retiring stereotypes, but some of my library colleagues are among the bravest people I've known. "Courageous librarians" didn't make the Coulee News article "10 Myths About Libraries and Librarians" a few years back, though. The Coulee list included bald myths such as "public libraries are only being busy during the school year," that "librarians are all fast readers" and "enjoy lots of time to read on the job," etc.

Coulee News also left "librarians know everything" off the myth list. However, once you're a librarian, you're tainted for life, and a surprising number of people harbor an unwarranted faith in my knowledge base and recall abilities; I'm lousy at Trivial Pursuits. Even aged public librarians are nothing if not service-oriented, so when a friend asked for the origin of a word, I answered the call. It was something of a special case. The inquisitor was Jennifer Jolis, director of Stone Soup Kitchens. For decades I've seen Jennifer put her money and time where her mouth is when it comes to improving our community and state. Recently Jennifer asked my sweetie, a Stone Soup volunteer, if I knew the origin of the term "rapscallion." I often don't have a clue about such things off the top of my head, but I do know where to look.

Jennifer's a culinary guru, and I hoped that "scallions" had something to do with cooking, but alas. The Oxford English Dictionary says "rapscallion," means a "rascal, rogue, vagabond, scamp," it dates from the late 1600s and comes from an earlier word with the same meaning, "rascallion," which was first cited in 1649. That appears to come from "rascal," which meant, chronologically speaking, a "young, lean, or inferior deer (1399)," "one belonging to the rabble or the common herd (1461)," a "low, mean, unprincipled, or dishonest fellow (1586)," a "a mild term of reproof (1610)." There's also "rascaless," a female rascal, and a "rascability" is a rabble.

"Rascal" is inordinately rich in potential suffixes that fairly trip along the tongue, including "rascalry," meaning "rascality," "rascalism: the character or practices of a rascal," and "rascaldom: the world or body of rascals." The world of rascals contains a few prominent librarians, like that horrid anti-Semite and sexual predator Melvil Dewey. Don't forget J. Edgar Hoover, Mao Tse Tung, and Elvis Presley, who all labored among the stacks at some point, though the King's time there was rather brief. But, as mentioned earlier, once a librarian...

The hands-down winner for rascal librarians is Giacomo Casanova, renowned Venetian lover and adventurer who also maintained catalogues and checked the stacks for mis-shelvings, albeit after his libido began to wane. His autobiography, "Story of My Life," is a diverting read, as well as one of the best sources on 18th century European social life, for besides a multitude of ladies, Casanova hung out with Voltaire, Goethe, and Mozart, as well as various kings and popes. He also orchestrated his own prison break, established the first state-run lottery, and practiced alchemy in search of the so-called "philosopher's stone" before being employed as librarian for the Bohemian Count Waldstein and writing his memoirs, for back then librarians with spare time wasn't a myth.

Casanova might not have been the best librarian, but he was among the most entertaining. As singer Debbie Harry put it, "You always fall for the rascal or the guy who's got a little bit of the devil in him."

Phantoms, Idiots, and Restrooms

Old Fort Phantom's remains stand on a rise just north of Abilene, Texas, where I grew up. We boys usually mispronounced it "fathom," which is an ancient British term meaning "two arms outstretched," in the sense of encircling with one's arms, and evolved into a nautical measure of six feet's length. Fort Phantom was far from the sea and deep in Indian country when it was established on Phantom Hill in 1852. As the overview at **FortPhantom.org** relates, life was hard and the fort was abandoned two years later. Nevertheless, settlers kept moving into the Comacheria, the huge area stretching from central Texas deep into New Mexico, Colorado, and Nebraska that was dominated by the fierce Comanches. So in 1858 Fort Phantom was re-established as a stagecoach station and Army "subpost." Only a few stone structures remain, but its ruins made a glorious playground for imaginative kids.

How Phantom Hill got its name is debatable. The way I heard it from creditable sources, the first settler's wife was exasperated by her husband's continual desire to keep going over the next rise searching for the perfect ranch site. She said his perfect ranch was a phantom, so he stopped and named their ranch "Phantom." My wife has noted similar occurrences even today, and objective observers must concede "Men Can Really Be Idiots." That's the subtitle of a Washington Post article about a British report, "Sex Differences in Idiotic Behavior," that analyzed the nominees of the

Darwin Award that's given posthumously to people who die "in such monumentally idiotic ways that the human race…is better off without them in the gene pool." For example, one winner was the "terrorist who mailed a letter bomb, and when it was returned for insufficient postage, opened it."

The "Male Idiot Theory," or MIT, study corroborated studies showing "men get into more car crashes than women. They're admitted to Emergency Rooms for accidents and injuries more often… They're more likely to drive fast, to commit crime, to climb mountains, sky dive, use drugs, take risks, and act impulsively." We fellas are seemingly wired that way. "Presumably," the study's authors noted, "idiotic behavior confers some, as yet unidentified, selective advantage on those who do not become its casualties."

MIT exacerbates another male phenomenon: bathroom humor proclivity. Bathroom activities provide disproportionate amusement for guys of all ages. However, age apparently blunts some of the MIT's impulsiveness, so I'll only mention three of the "9 Surprising Facts About Flatulence You May Not Know" that Joseph Stromberg wrote about for **Vox.com**. First, "99 percent of the gas you produce does not smell" because most of it results from swallowed air instead of bacteria off-gassing. Secondly, drinking carbonated beverages and chewing gum enhances the phenomenon.

Third, beware of Beano. It reduces gas production by utilizing an enzyme called "alpha-galactosidase" that digests carbohydrates in your small intestine before arriving in the large intestine, where your bacterial pals are waiting to ferment them. Our personal microbiome, the microorganisms inside us that outnumber our human cells ten-to-one, are actually starved by Beano overuse. Recent research is revealing how this little-known part of our anatomies is necessary for good health. Anyone with chronic digestive problems should read "The Excrement Experiment" by Emily Eakin in the December 1, 2015 New Yorker magazine. It's enlightening, disgusting, and available through the library's databases at **fnsblibrary.org**.

Decades of wrestling with public restroom behaviors and design make it impossible to not notice advances like "odor-eating toilet seats" being introduced by the Kohler Company and the existence of the Sulabh International Museum of Toilets in India. The former's pretty self-explanatory, involving fans and scent-pads, while the latter educates "students about the historical trends in the development of toilets."

Vandalism at our library's restroom dropped an estimated 80 percent when it was remodeled a few years ago with increased lighting, timed toilets and faucets, and stainless steel everywhere. Paper towels tempt some fools to stop up the sinks and toilets, so Dyson airblades were installed that push water off recently-washed hands while saving energy over loud, inefficient, evaporative blowers. The culprits are seldom discovered, unlike their messes. As Virginia Woolfe noted, "It is far harder to kill a phantom than a reality."

Bad Boys and Girls, Who's Who, and Mr. Toilet

···

"**W**hat's in a name?" Shakespeare once asked, and that's what School Stickers, a British company, wanted to know, too. School Stickers sells motivational stickers to teachers and offers a service that "tracks children's behavior and digitally rewards ones for behaving well." 56,000 students were involved last year, and, according to the survey results on the **www.SchoolStickers.com** webpage, "Jacob, Daniel, Thomas, James and Adam are the names of the best behaved boys, but Joseph, Cameron, William, Jake, and Joshua need to shape up. Amy, Georgia, Emma, Charlotte, and Grace are the names of the best behaved girls, while Ella, Bethany, Eleanor, Olivia, and Laura" weren't.

Hey! Don't kill the messenger! As School Stickers' Managing Director Neil Hodges, said, "The annual Santa's Naughty and Nice List is just a bit of fun." Along those same lines, consider the title of Steven Levitt's 2006 **Freakanomics.com** article: "The Next Time Your Daughter Brings Home a New Boyfriend, Be Sure To Ask His Middle Name." A reader sent Levitt a large number of clippings from six months of the Dallas Morning News that all featured horrible crimes committed by people who shared the middle name "Wayne." Back in 1996 the **NewsOfTheWeird.com** site began running lists of accused murderers all with the middle name Wayne.

William Wayne Justice, on the other hand, was one of the great progressive legal minds in Texas history, and Ima Hogg, daughter of Governor Jim Hogg, was a truly great person and philanthropist, so what's in a name? Few non-Germans crave the name "Hansel," yet it's also a noun for "a gift of good luck given at the beginning of the new year." Those with open minds who dare can check out the library's copy of "John Train's Most Remarkable Names." Among Train's documented names on page 57 alone you'll find not only the twins Halloween and Easter Buggage and Houston, Texas undertaker Groaner Digger, but also Gretel von Garlic of New York City.

Albert Marquis was once a big name in names. He founded "Marquis' Who's Who in America" in 1899, a half-century after the British invented the concept, which was initially only a list of prominent people. In 1897 the Brits began including more detailed biographical information, and Marquis was inspired. So were many copycats. Our public library's collection includes Who's Who books in fields ranging from American art, the Bible, cartoon actor voices, outer space, opera, country music, oil spill prevention, golf, jazz, mythology, pop culture, World War II, "people in line to the British throne," and a slew of literary ones, like who's who in Shakespeare, and Zane Grey, and science fiction.

Then there are the scams. One type preys on the ignorant to get their credit card and other personal information through interviews and promises of being included in a swanky-looking book. Some folks seek out these impressive-looking publications for vanity and business reasons. There are European who's who books that will for a price certify your family as pure nobility.

So you have to admire a guy that embraces the nickname "Mr. Toilet." Jack Sim is an entrepreneur in Singapore who decided to make the world a better place by improving global sanitation. He spearheads a number of projects, particularly the WTO, or World Toilet Organization. He's even written and produced two feature-length movies, "Everybody's Business" and "Life Without Toilets," the latter filmed in Bollywood complete with songs and dance. India is also home to the Sulabh International Museum of Toilets, a museum dedicated to educating the ignorant about historical trends in toilet development.

Surely that museum has copies of the "2009-2014 Outlook for Wood Toilet Seats in Greater China." You can buy a copy from Amazon for only $495, and that's a bargain compared to the "2007-2012 World Outlook for Wood Toilet Seats," which runs $795. At least check out the Amazon listing for the book's customer reviews. They're obviously fake, but hilarious. For example, "All I did was look at the cover, but I already knew from the start, this is, without a doubt, still a better story than 'Twilight.'"

There's no better place to figure out who's who than your public library, where even the Camerons, Olivias, and Waynes of the world are welcome to learn. As long as they behave!

Torture, Webster's, and That That

....

Judging by our national debate over the subject, "torture" is one of those terms whose meaning seems to depend on who's using or hearing it. Much of the rationale for condoning torture for interrogation seems couched in "syntactic ambiguity," which is a long way of saying "amphibology," which is defined by Webster's as "a sentence or phrase (as 'nothing is good enough for you') that can be interpreted in more than one way." An extreme example can be found in "Brewer's Dictionary of Phrase & Fable," that bottomless source of intellectual whimsy, which cites a poem about proper usage of the word "That"

"For be it known that we may safely write/ Or say that 'that THAT' that that man wrote was right;/ Nay e'en that that THAT, that 'that THAT' has followed,/ Through six repeats, the grammar's rule has hallowed;/ And that that THAT that THAT 'that THAT' began /Repeated seven times is right, deny't who can." Another example designed to illustrate the importance of punctuation is "That that is is that that is not is not is that it it is." Or "That that is, is. That that is not, is not. Is that it? It is." For some language-lovers, this stuff is ecstasy, but for others, it's torturous.

When Webster was cited above, everyone knew who was meant: Daniel Webster, the father of American lexicography and creator of the first great American dictionary. He published a trial one in 1806, but it took him another 22 years to complete the first edition of his American Dictionary of the English Language. It contained over 70,000 definitions, 30,000 more than Samuel "Dictionary" Johnson's famous dictionary published the century before. To accomplish this feat Webster learned 26 languages, including Old English, Greek, and Sanskrit. Sadly, only 2,500 copies of Webster's 1828 dictionary sold, and he mortgaged his home to put out the second edition in 1840 and then died three years later.

Webster urged reforming the strange spellings of some words from the mother country. He succeeded with some, like "ax," "color," and "center," but his efforts to promote "wimmin," "dawter," and "tung" fizzled. Others are worth reconsidering today: "after-wise," meaning "wise afterwards or too late," "packthread," meaning "strong string to tie parcels," and "tardigradous," meaning "slow-paced," all seem eminently efficient and useful terms. Webster included many great S-words, such as to "sheep-bite," ("practice petty thefts"), "scranch" ("grind with the teeth"), and "squabbish" ("thick, fat, heavy"). And don't forget his "babblement," meaning "senseless prattle or unmeaning words."

"The Web of Language" is a interesting language-related blog written by University of Illinois professor Dennis Baron. In a recent entry Baron suggested that "torture" should be considered by a candidate by some of the word-of-the-year (WOTY) compilers. He noted that "December brought 'enhanced interrogation techniques, or EITs, back into our vocabulary. This euphemism for torture resurfaced with the Senate Intelligence Committee's report on CIA detention and questioning of terror suspects...it's the epitome of what went wrong, not just with counterterrorism, but with everything."

Baron noted how Samuel Johnson chose "internets" ("any virtual system of nodes reticulated or decussated, at equal distances, with interstices at the intersection") as the word of the year for 1755, when his Dictionary of the English Language was published. "Not to be outdone," Baron wrote, "Webster nominated 'torture' for the best word of 1828, defining it in...terms that could have come right out of a Bush White House memorandum: 'Severe pain inflicted judicially, either as a punishment for a crime, or for the purpose of extorting a confession from an accused person."

For the record, in 2014 Merriam-Webster's WOTY was "culture." In Germany it was "Lichtgrenze," which means "border of light, a display commemorating the fall of the Berlin Wall." Reflecting the times, Norway's WOTY was "Fremmedkriger," or "foreign fighter," and the "Dutch picked 'Dagobertducktaks,' a 'Scrooge McDuck' tax on the rich."

As a counterbalance to tortuous amphibology everywhere, my WOTY is "concinnity," "harmonious arrangement of various parts," which also describes a well-run library." You can quickly tell upon entering a library if it's arranged more for the librarian's ease and happiness than those using it. When that happens, it's pure torture.

Poprocks, Paraprosdokians, and Kindness

Voltaire's 18th century warning remains valid. "It is dangerous," he wrote, "to be right in matters on which the established authorities are wrong." And it's mighty easy to get things wrong. One of the popular books featured in the just-completed local Guys Read program was "National Geographic's Kids Myths Busted," which clarified a variety of misassumptions. For instance, the average person does not swallow four spiders in their sleep annually, or even one, eating Poprocks while drinking a soda won't make you explode, and pennies dropped from the Empire State Building won't kill someone on the sidewalk. However, a ballpoint pen, with its aerodynamic shape, can reach 200 mph when dropped from that height.

Other examples of getting things wrong have arisen in linguistic and rhetorician circles over paraprosdokians. The arrival of "10 Paraprosdokians To Tickle Your Brain" brought the term to my attention. The accompanying definition said "paraprosdokians are figures of speech where the latter part of the phrase is humorously surprising or unexpected and causes the reader or listener to reframe or reinterpret the first part." Dorothy Parker was a past master at them, such as "If all the girls who attended the Yale prom were laid end to end, I wouldn't be a bit surprised."

Never encountering a paraprosdokian before, I looked in **Outlook.com**, my turn-to word-related web resource, but out of its 1,061 dictionaries, only five listed paraprosdokian, including the unreliable Worthless Word of the Day Dictionary and Urban Dictionary. The "Glossary of Rhetorical Terms with Examples" appeared authoritative because its link produced the University of Kentucky's Classics Graduate Program website that claimed this glossary originated with a professor at Wayne State University.

Besides paraprosdokian, the glossary included better-known parts of speech, like irony. However, a little research unearthed "The Bogus Word 'Paraprosdokian' and the Lazy Con men of Academe" by Canadian lexicographer Bill Cassleman. Cassleman's hackles were raised by professors acting as if paraprosdokian was a classical word "sanctioned by centuries of use," and not the freshly-coined neologism that it is. Paraprosdokian, he writes, "appears NOWHERE in ancient Greek literature. It could NEVER be an ancient Greek word with its Late Latin adjectival ending –ian! It has never been listed in any edition of the Oxford English Dictionary."

Everyone wants true, lasting love, so the recent Atlantic article by Emily Esfahani Smith titled "Science Says Lasting Relationships Come Down to 2 Basic Traits," was a must-read. It cited research by University of Washington psychologist John Gottmann, founder of the Gottman Institute that's "devoted to helping couples build and maintain loving, healthy relationships based on scientific studies." It's a fascinating and convincing article that describes how Gottman established "The Love Lab" to study how newlywed couples interact. The lovers' heart rates, sweating, and other physiological reactions were tracked as they discussed how they met, as well as their negative and positive memories. Couples who were supportive and responsive to their partners had lower metabolic rates, while the rates of couples who were rude or inconsiderate were much higher.

Gottman determined that the couples most likely to support or simply acknowledge each other's comments did so 90% of the time, while those who didn't respond positively did so 33% of the time. In other words, "Contempt...is the number one factor that tears couples apart. People who are focused on criticizing their partners miss a whopping 50% of positive things their partners are doing, and they see negativity when it's not there... Being mean is the death knell of a relationship. Kindness, on the other hand glues couples together...kindness (along with emotional stability) is the most important predictor of satisfaction and stability in a marriage... there's a great deal of evidence showing that more someone receives or witnesses kindness, the more they will be kind themselves."

In short, those who look for goodness find it, and so do those looking for badness. It's what separates censors from public library book selectors, who look for good books rather than guard against bad ones. Opinions about good and bad will always vary. But Ogden Nash was right when he said, "To keep your marriage brimming / With love in the loving cup, / Whenever you're wrong admit it; / Whenever you're right, shut up."

Secrets of Painters, Bank Robbers, and Social Workers

....

"We don't make mistakes, just happy little accidents," was one of many Zen-like observations of Bob Ross, host of PBS' "The Joy of Painting" series that ran from 1983 to 1994. Regular PBS viewers encountered Ross' program and his bubbly, up-beat banter, not to mention his ubiquitous frizzy afro hair-do. But Ross was also a man of secrets. For instance, despite his soft voice and gentle approach that had critics comparing him to Fred Rogers, Ross was an Air Force master sergeant. As he told an interviewer, "I was the guy who makes you scrub the latrine...who screams at you for being late to work. The job requires you to be a mean, tough person. And I was fed up with it."

Ross was assigned to Eielson AFB near Fairbanks and was inspired by Interior Alaska's natural beauty. During breaks from work he developed his famed quick-painting techniques to produce artwork. After retiring from the military, Ross produced his "Joy of Painting" TV program for free, relying on his art supply and instructional company for income. He made over 30,000 paintings, all of which he donated or gave away, except for goldpans he illustrated during his Eielson years that he sold for $25.

As Kahil Gibran noted, "If you reveal your secrets to the wind, you should not blame the wind for revealing them to the trees." That didn't inhibit Ross, nor did it Alphonso Jennings, a bank and train robber, and a lawyer, in the late 1800s, who later made several silent movies about his exploits to deter others from a life of crime. "The Bank Robbery" of 1908, a silent movie classic, recreated one of Jennings' hold-ups, and it inspired him to write, produce and star in "The Lady of the Dugout," which is included on our public library's copy of "Treasures 5: The West" DVD. The Turner Classic Movie Database said the film co-starred Jennings' and his brother Frank and "is surprisingly honest in its depictions of these two men. It doesn't try to hide the fact that they were bank robbers or that they injured people during their criminal acts... 'The Lady of the Dugout' is a rather remarkable film, filled with fascinating characters and emotional twists and turns."

Jennings was eventually pardoned by Teddy Roosevelt, ran a strong race for Oklahoma governor, and then toured with his film, proselytizing about avoiding a life of crime. The notes on the DVD told how Jennings was captured and imprisoned, and his cell-mate turned out to be none other than William Porter, who's better known as author O. Henry. Jennings wrote his autobiography, "Beating Back," and later with Henry co-penned a book about their friendship titled, "Through the Shadows with O. Henry'. Both pre-date the 1923 cut-off for copyright protection, so I downloaded free e-book versions using the library's WIFI, which is much quicker than my sluggardly home connection in the woods, and found them both entertaining reads, especially after watching "Lady of the Dugout."

AMightyGirl.com is a great source for feisty, women-related history. There I recently read about another secretive person: Irena Sendler, a nurse, social worker and "one of the great unsung heroes of WWII who led a secret operation to successfully smuggle 2,500 Jewish children out of the Warsaw Ghetto." Sendler was head of the children's division of the Zegota, the Polish resistance organization. Her day job in the Polish government's Social Welfare Department allowed her to inspect Jewish children for typhus, enabling her to smuggle them out of the ghetto in potato sacks, coffins, and an ambulance with a false bottom. What's more, Sendler compiled lists of the children and their locations and buried them in jars to facilitate reuniting survivors after the war.

Sendler was caught, imprisoned, tortured, and sentenced to death. "Fortunately, the Zegota was able to bribe the German guards as she was on her way to execution," and she successfully hid until war's end. Her exploits were mostly forgotten until 1999, when three American high school girls undertook a year-long history project. Starting with a brief news clipping about Sendler, they wound up writing a play about her, "Life in a Jar" and inspired greater interest in Sendler's achievements, including books and a documentary.

Sendler's fortitude and achievement were amazing. But as Bob Ross, pointed out, "the secret to doing anything is believing that you can do it."

Counting Words, Appreciating Hyphens, and Loathing Lowth

Every word counts in the world of publishing. Successful short stories writers make less than novelists, since their work amounts to 1,000 to 7,500 words, according to Lee Masterson's **FictionFactor.com**, "the online magazine for fiction writers." She says 100-word-or-less "micro-fiction," an "abbreviated story is often difficult to write, and even harder to write well... Pay rates are often low, but for so few words, the rate per word average quite high." "Flash fiction," one-page stories of 100–1,000 words are in between micro- and short stories. "In most cases," Masterson wrote, "industry standard preferred length is 250 words per page, so a 400 page novel would be about 100,000 words."

The 250 standard originated in the days of manual typewriters. Modern word processors have all sorts of fat and skinny fonts, but the 250-word standard harkens to earlier, simpler times, just like the "return" that's still printed on many computer keyboard's "enter" button. Fortunately for our peace of mind, the "Courier New 12 pt." font, usually the default typeface for Microsoft Word and others, averages 250 words per page.

Writing about word counts provides double pleasure. First, this column has been restricted to 700 words for many years, and this has forced more economical writing upon me, though it occasionally fosters some grammatical conniving. Second, the hyphen, that transformer of two words into one, is my ally, and I employ it enthusiastically. Masterson's article provided ample hyphenating opportunities. However, some old stick-in-the-muds, like The Chicago Manual of Style, recommend "a spare hyphenation style." I can't argue when the CMS says "to hyphenate only if doing so will aid readability," but I suspect I might define "readability" differently from the CMS.

I inherited writing this column back in Seguin, Texas 30-some-odd years ago when I was installed as the public library director there and told that was part of the duties. However, I didn't want to take the usual "what's new at the library," hoping instead to lure the unwary from library-related ignorance with amusement. Working in an active library provides a never-ending flow of facts, concepts, and fancies, so I decided to pass some of those along to potential readers while slipping in a bit about libraries here and there.

Originally there was no word count limit. At my second library's town newspaper, it was 1,400 words, and those loosey-goosey columns are embarrassing to read today. Some 1,500 columns later, my writing's improved some, but there's often more that I want to share that won't fit in the 700-word allotment. Pictures often help illuminate text, so I've added illustrations to several year's-worth of these columns at my blog, **HillofBooks.org**. New ones appear there a day or so after running in the News Miner.

Fortunately or unfortunately, I've always written in isolation from the newsroom and consequently only occasionally hear the faintest of editorial rumblings. Still, the many editors who've scrutinized my scribblings have been kind about my persistent use of "y'all" for the second person plural, not to mention countless dangling participles and the like. But, dang it, sometimes colloquialisms read better than "proper English." I enjoyed a recent **Economist. com** article by "R.L.G." titled "A Long Decline," about the imminent, yet never forthcoming, collapse of English. It begins by quoting William Langland, author of "Piers the Plowman" who died in 1386: "There is not a single modern schoolboy who can compose verses or write a decent letter." A Benedictine monk, Ramulph Higden, complained about the same thing in 1387, as did John Dryden in 1672, Jonathan Swift in the 1730s, and many others. Yet, English somehow continues to thrive.

In 1762 Anglican Bishop Robert Lowth published his "Short Introduction to English Grammar," which is considered one of the most influential grammar guides ever. Instead of merely describing grammar, Lowth tried to applied the strictures of Latin on our freewheeling tongue. It often didn't fit, that didn't stop Lowth from telling everyone how things ought to be. Sadly, many "experts" went along with him for the next 150 years. That's right: he's the guy who came up with the anti-dangling participle rule, among a slew of others, ironically stating, "this is an idiom which our language is strongly inclined to."

He also had the temerity to castigate the writings of Shakespeare, John Milton, and the King James Bible, some of the noblest ever penned, for "false syntax." One might say he's easy to loathe.

Library Litotes, Data-Overload, and the Pollyanna Hypothesis

....

There are more than a few books in our public library, and the print books aren't going away anytime soon. Both statements are true, and both are excellent examples of litotes, an "ironical understatement" according to **OxfordDictionaries.com,** "in which an affirmative is expressed by the negative of its contrary (e.g., 'you won't be sorry')." However, in David Levitin's "The Organized Mind," published last August, it's estimated that "We live in a world with 300 exabytes (300 billion billion bytes) of information...yet the capacity of the conscious mind is a mere 120 bits per second. This presents a challenge not only to our processing capacity, but also our decision-making ability... In 2011 Americans took in five times as much information every day as they did in 1986—the equivalent of 175 newspapers."

Unfortunately, this also presents a plethora of little moment-to-moment decisions: do I read this next? Should I check my messages? Or choose this website over that one? Levitin noted that "One of the most useful findings in recent neuroscience could be summed up as: 'The decision-making network in our brain doesn't prioritize.'" In other words, unlike breathing and swallowing, decision-making doesn't happen automatically; we have to consciously make up our minds to do it. But, "During our leisure time, not counting work, each of us processes 34 gigabytes or 100,000 words every day."

These thoughts might be occasioned by the annual Patrick O'Brian binge I feel coming on, for O'Brian possessed an amazing and amusing vocabulary that's displayed frequently is his 7,000-page Aubrey-Maturin series of novels set in Napoleonic times. Whatever the impetus, lately I've noticed increasingly frequent mentions of nautically-based words. For example, **DailyWritingTips.com**, my regular resource for honing my grammar, has recently compared definitions and uses of "gibe, gybe, jibe, and jive," and threw in "jerry-rigged and jury-rigged" for good measure. To be succinct, "gibe," dating from the 1570s, are taunts while a "gybe," which comes from 17th century Dutch word "giben," occurs when a sail suddenly shifts from one side of a boat to the other." "Jive" can mean "a type of fast, lively jazz," "uninhibited dancing," or "talk that is false, misleading, or worthless."

"Jury-rigged" originated with the "jury-mast, a nautical term for a temporary mast put in place of one that's been broken or blown away" and, in this context "jury" is "of uncertain origin," according to the Online Etymological Dictionary. The same source says that "jerry-rigged," or "jerry-built," was first used in 1869 to mean "bad, defective." The origin of "jerry-rigged" is also lost to time, but, according to **DailyWritingTips.com**. "A jerry-builder was a contractor who put up shoddy houses for a quick sale. The first citation for the adjective jerry-built houses is dated 1869."

As a species we loathe using such negative connotations. In a **ScienceDaily.com** article last month, University of Vermont researchers announced that they might have proven the validity of the "Pollyanna Hypothesis" that "there is a universal tendency to use positive words more frequently than negative ones. 'Put even more simply,' they wrote, 'humans tend to look on (and talk about) the bright side of life.'" The Pollyanna Hypothesis originated in 1969 at the University of Illinois, and with that era's limited technology for broadly surveying language usage, it remained mostly hypothetical until the Vermont scientists hooked up with the MITRE Corporation, a nonprofit engineering and technology organization.

Backed by a National Science Foundation grant they "gathered billions of words from around the world using twenty-four types of sources, including books, news outlets, social media, websites, television and movie subtitles, and music lyrics. For example, we collected roughly one hundred billion words in tweets." They then "identified about ten thousand of the most frequently-used words in each of ten languages: English, Spanish, French, German, Brazilian Portuguese, Korean, Chinese, Russian, Indonesian, and Arabic." Native speakers were paid to rate all the frequently-used words on a 1-9 happiness scale. For comparison, in English, "laughter" rated 8.50, "the" 4.98, and "terrorist" 1.30.

"In all cases, the scientists found 'a usage-invariant positivity bias'… In other words, by looking at the words people actually use most often they found that, on average, we—humanity—use more happy words than sad words." So cheer up, for as Abraham Lincoln noted, "Most folks are as happy as they make up their minds to be."

Pronouns, Pseudonyms, and the Curiosolites

....

Humans just have to name the objects and creatures we encounter, including ourselves. How we choose those names, even pronouns, like "I," "you," and "them" is interesting. For instance, how do you talk to yourself when stressed? "Pronouns Matter When Psyching Yourself Up," a recent Harvard Business Review article, noted that "Some people seem to have an amazing ability to stay rational no matter what...while the rest of us waste energy doing things like panicking about upcoming tasks." Researchers from Harvard, Michigan State, and UC Berkley have carried out experiments that reveal a major key to keeping cool is how you name yourself.

They found that when talking to themselves, some people refer to themselves in the first person, using "I" or "me," as in "what am I going to do now?" They're also more likely to fold up under pressure than those who refer to themselves using a second- or third-person pronoun, as in "what are you going to do now?", or by their personal name. The studies showed that we perform significantly better under duress if we've psyched ourselves up beforehand with a pep talk that omits using the pronouns "I" or "me."

There are other ways we think of, and present, ourselves. Some writers employ pen names, for example. In that regard no one has equaled Daniel DeFoe, author of "Robinson Crusoe" and no less than 545 novels, poems, and pamphlets, many under amusing pseudonyms. DeFoe, whose real name was "Foe," wrote political screeds of any persuasion if the money was right. He boasted of having at least 198 pseudonyms, including gems like, "Anti-bubbler," "Betty Blueskin," "Count Kidney-Face," "Tom Manywife," "Furioso," and "Tea-Table."

Ebenezer Cobham Brewer thought of himself as "the Compiler." After graduating from Cambridge and being ordained, Brewer returned to the family home and an uncertain future. However, he continued his favorite hobby. "I have always read with a slip of paper and a pencil at my side, to jot down whatever I think may be useful to me," he wrote, "and these jottings I keep sorted in different lockers. This has been a life-habit with me."

In 1838, the year he moved home, Brewer compiled some of these notes into "A Guide to the Scientific Knowledge of Things Familiar." It was published and became a bestseller and funded his subsequent extensive European travels. A prodigious reader, Brewer published another compilation, "The Readers Handbook of Allusions, References, Plots, and Stories," in 1896, the year before his death. His magnum opus, or greatest work, was "Brewer's Dictionary of Phrase & Fable," which is reverentially known among generations of reference librarians simply as "Brewer's. He intended it for the 19th century's growing numbers of literate people who didn't have advanced educations but wanted to comprehend the allusions and references made by the educated classes. The first few editions were, as described by Wikipedia, "highly idiosyncratic, with certain editorial decisions highly suggestive of the author's personal bias."

New, updated editions of "Brewer's" are still being published. Now known as the "Dictionary of Modern Phrase & Fable, 19th edition," its current editor, Susie Dent, says, "it is not just a reference book, nor is it a single read; it is not entirely objective…it is not a straightforward dictionary, nor is it an encyclopedia. It is, in fact, unlike any other reference book that exists, anywhere.

But, oh, what a joy to browse! It's a hefty, squat book, and every page is packed with intriguing entries. For instance, looking up

"Samhain" pronounced "sown, like "gown," (the Celtic celebration of the harvest and beginning of their new year, which evolved into our Halloween) on page 1218, I found "Sam Hill" ("A US euphemism for 'hell'), "Sampford Ghost" ("An uncommonly persistent poltergeist that haunted a thatched house...for about three years until 1810), and "The Samian Letter" ("The letter Y, used by Pythagoras as an emblem of the straight narrow path of virtue"), among others.

Although occasionally something of an "ultracrepidarian," or "one who gives opinions beyond one's area of expertise," I believe Brewer's slipped in neglecting the Curiosolites, a Celtic tribe on coastal France that sounded a promising place for librarians. But the Celts were illiterate. It's more fun being a librarian among those book-loving Alaskans.

Confusing English, Difficult Reading, and Bad Politics

The Atlantic Monthly is such a good magazine that I subscribe to it, even though I can read it, and even check it out, at our public library. The reason is Atlantic has such well-written, informative and in-depth articles that really grab and inform my attention. A case in point is "How Spelling Keeps Kids From Learning" by Luba Vangelova. Published last February, this article points out that "written English is great for puns but terrible for learning to read and write" due to its innumerable inconsistencies. "Adults who have already mastered written English tend to forget about its many quirks," Vangelova wrote. "But consider this: English has 205 ways to spell 44 sounds. And not only can the same sounds be represented in different ways, but the same letter or letter combinations can also correspond to different sounds."

A study by the English Spelling Society found that of the 7,000 most common English words, 60% had one or more unpredictable letters. Finnish, by comparison, has few exceptions to its straightforward spelling rules. Finnish has "a nearly one-to-one correspondence between sounds and letters, meaning fewer rules to learn. So after Finnish children learn their alphabet, learning to read is pretty straightforward—they can read well within three months of starting formal learning... A 2003 study found that English-speaking children typically needed about three years to master the basics of reading and writing, whereas their counterparts in most European countries needed a year or less." Vangelova wrote, quoting the study, "In countries like Finland, children continue to improve their vocabulary and use of language...but because they spell by rules rather than by imprinting the right look of words on their brains, they can spell any word, regardless of whether they have met it before or not."

English is so hard that it engenders a greater proportion of functionally illiterate citizens, who "cannot read or write well enough for everyday literacy needs... Maybe they've learned enough to cope with simple items such as menus, but they still struggle deciphering lengthy prose passages and reading important documents." Three-fourths of welfare recipients are functionally illiterate, as are over 60% of the prison population. "All in all, according to the Literacy Project Foundation, illiteracy costs American taxpayers about $20 billion a year."

Changing pronunciations and the introduction of foreign words caused many of English's inconsistencies, but a major reason for them dates from the 1400s and the birth of printing. The first English-language printing press was run by Belgians who didn't speak English, and the first Bibles were printed by other European printers with equally poor grasps of English. These guys were paid by the line, so they found ways to pad things a bit, like adding extra letters to words. That's why "frend" became "friend." Then Samuel Johnson's great Dictionary of 1755 came out with loads of alternate spellings of words, Noah Webster's 1828 dictionary contained all sorts of Americanized spellings, and no one ever got around to reforming all the differences.

So learning effective English is daunting, but it's absolutely mandatory for successfully negotiating pathways to successful living. Teaching reading and writing is a delicate and difficult process, too. Drilling kids to read doesn't work, but inspiring them to read certainly does. "Reading should not be presented to children as a chore or duty. It should be offered to them as a precious gift," as Kate

DiCamillo said. But that takes teaching time that's too often spent in training students how to take standardized tests. Dry, repetitive, formulaic reading instruction actually diminishes students' ability to recall details of what they've read, according to a **ScienceDaily. com** article, "Learning By Repetition Impairs Recall of Details." Meanwhile, fostering the joy of discovering the world through the printed word produces readers and productive, contributing citizens. It's a no-brainer.

So why are elected officials so quick to embrace draconian slashing of education and library budgets? That sort of thinking is foolish and shortsighted, and, as a direct result, our state and communities will become poorer in day-to-day living skills, employable work forces, future prospects, and overall quality of life. "Reading is important," children's author Tomie de Paola noted, "because if you can read, you can learn anything about everything and everything about anything."

Etymological Enticements, Origins of Scoundrels, and Casey Gets a Hit

R alph Waldo Emerson described his fellow fanciers of word origins this way: "The etymologist finds the deadest words to have been once a brilliant picture. Language is fossil poetry." I'm also fascinated by how words reflect what life was once like, but I'm more dabbler than linguist. Nevertheless, librarians seem to persistently carry the onus of deep knowledge, like preachers being automatically assumed to be spiritual. I'm no dynamo at Trivial Pursuit, but while I often don't know the answers to questions posed out of the blue, I usually know where to look.

Take "scoundrel," for example. I'm an eager student at many Osher Lifelong Learning Institute classes, including "Scoundrels in Northern History," a history course that's led by Dave Norton. One of my classmates asked Dave where the word "scoundrel" comes from, and he deferred to the nearest librarian, me, who was absolutely clueless. But knew where to find the clues. "Scoundrel" is defined in the Oxford English Dictionary and Black's Law Dictionary, among other reputable sources. I own the Compact OED, which comes with a magnifying glass due to its tiny print, and found "scoundrel" defined as "an audacious rascal, one destitute of all moral scruple." Calling the public library reference staff (459-1046) produced Black's definition ("an opprobrious epithet implying rascality, villainy, or a want of honor"), and the knowledge that calling someone a scoundrel isn't actionable as slander.

My copy of Eric Partridge's "Origins: A Short Etymological Dictionary of Modern English agrees that "scoundrel" is "of obscure origin," but said it was analogous with "wastrel" in the Anglo-French word "escoundre," which came from the Old French "escondre." Whatever its origin, there are some wonderful related quotes I can't argue with, such as George Bernard Shaw's "Every man over forty is a scoundrel," and Samuel Johnson's "Whoever thinks of going to bed before midnight is a scoundrel."

Baseball season is upon us, and that game's possessed plenty of interesting scoundrels, from the Black Sox on up to the beefy consumers of performance enhancing drugs. Sad to say, these include the former Goldpanners Jason Giambi and Barry Bonds. However, Giambi 'fessed up, cleaned up, and took his punishment, while Bonds hasn't, and will consequently never make the Baseball Hall of Fame. Although baseball's arrival is a perennial harbinger of spring, rebirth, and renewed hope, let's look at the scoundrels behind "Casey at the Bat."

"The outlook was brilliant for the Mudville nine that day," Ernest Thayer's poem begins, "The score stood four to two, with but one more inning to play." By the way, "inning," according to the **OnlineEtymology.com**, comes from the Old English "innung," which meant "a taking in, a putting in." It was first used as "a team's turn in a game" in reference to cricket in 1735 and was later adopted by American baseball.

I read in **HistoryBuff.com** that Thayer invented Casey for the San Francisco Examiner, being hired by William Randolph Hearst, the newspaper's new twenty-something publisher, who previously had edited the Harvard Lampoon, and whose father gave him the Examiner upon graduating from Harvard. W.R. Hearst brought along three fellow Lampoon editors to the Examiner, including Thayer, who contributed regular humor pieces under his pseudonym, "Phin."

One piece was "Casey at the Bat," published June 3, 1888. However, no one noticed the poem until it was republished in the New York Sun several weeks later who attributed it to "Anonymous." This article was clipped out by Archibald Gunter, a novelist who regularly scoured newspapers for ideas. When Gunter read in August 1888 that the New York and Chicago baseball teams would attend a performance by his friend, comedian De Wolf Hopper, he gave his copy of "Casey" to Hopper for his act, and the poem was a huge hit on stage. Hopper performed it regularly thereafter, and three ink-stained scoundrels subsequently claimed authorship, but couldn't prove it. Five years later Thayer, the antithesis of scoundreldom, returned East and attended Hopper's show, heard his poem, and afterwards gave the comedian royalty-free performance rights.

Legendary sportswriter Grantland Rice composed "Casey's Revenge" in 1908 that's more suited to the optimism of spring, when every team's a contender. "Oh somewhere in this favored land dark clouds may hide the sun;/ And somewhere bands no longer play and children have no fun;/ And somewhere over blighted loves there hangs a heavy pall;/ But Mudville hearts are happy now—for Casey hit the ball."

Pronouns Redux, Second-Person Y'all, and She-Who-Must-Be-Obeyed

....

Today's word is "redux," defined in the American Heritage Dictionary as "brought back, returned," because there's more to say about last week's column's theme: pronouns. For starters, the Swedish Academy announced they're adding "hen," a gender-neutral pronoun to fit between "han" and "hon," the Swedish "he" and "she." And for an amusing bedtime read, try Alexander McCall Smith's "Portuguese Irregular Verbs," featuring linguist "Professor Dr. von Igelfeld." Smith's better known for his "Ladies No. 1 Detective Agency" novels, but his von Igelfeld novels successfully and gently send up the academic world in fine, sleep-inducing fashion.

Meanwhile, the national embracing of "y'all" as our second person plural pronoun proceeds apace. An excellent description of how and why appeared in the **Slate.com** article by Alyssa Pelish, "Do You Say Y'all? How About Yous? The Second Person Plural Won't Be Ignored!" Fifth century Anglo Saxon words "'þu,' like 'thou,' addressed one person, and 'ge,' like 'ye' or 'you,' indicated more than one." Then Normans invaders brought polite and informal second person plurals. "In other words, 'ye' was used when speaking to an individual nobleman or a gathering of peasants. 'Thou' was reserved for an intimate or an inferior and was always singular."

By the mid-1500s "the language eventually rid itself completely of a class-based pronoun hierarchy…'you' started replacing all other second person pronouns and becoming an all-purpose means of address—number and social standing be damned." Shakespeare's "Twelfth Night," written around 1600, used "thou" and "you" interchangeably. A century later DeFoe's "Robinson Crusoe" saw "you" outnumbering "thou" eight-to-one. And Austen's "Sense and Sensibility" a century on used only "you" and with nary a "thou." Thus died the English second person plural pronoun, until "y'all" emerged out of necessity. Remember: one person is never "y'all." And several groups are "all y'all." As in, "Y'all come!" "But my mother-in-law is visiting." "Then all y'all come!"

Pronouns are ancient words. A 2009 BBC article titled "Oldest English Words Identified" cited a Reading University study that found "I" and "we" as "dating back tens of thousands of years." The researchers used supercomputers to identify "a lexicon of 200 words that is not specific to culture or technologies, and is therefore not likely to represent concepts that have changed across nations or millennia… What the researchers found was that the frequency with which a word is used relates to how slowly it changes through time, so that the most common words tend to be the oldest ones."

"Meanwhile, the fastest-changing words are projected to die out and be replaced by other words much sooner." There are 46 different ways of saying "dirty" in Indo-European languages, for example, so, odds are, "it is likely to die out soon in English, along with 'stick' and 'guts.' "

English literature has had its share of notable pronouns, too, such as Isaac Asimov's classic, "I, Robot," and Joyce Carol Oats' "Them." However, my favorite is a clerihew about Henry Rider Haggard, a moderately talented but extremely popular novelist from the 1880s to 1920s best known for novels "King Solomon's Mines" and "She." If you've read the latter, or, better yet, seen the movie, you'll recall that the title character's more formally known as "She-Who-Must-Be-Obeyed." That's also the name a Haggard childhood nurse gave "a disreputable doll of particularly hideous aspect" that she placed in his bedroom each night to watch and keep him quiet.

Clerihews shouldn't be confused with double dactyl, although both involve biographical information. **PoeticByway.com** says a dactyl is "a metrical foot of three syllables, the first of which is long or accented...as in 'MER-ily' or 'LOV-er boy'." The double dactyl consists of two quatrains with two dactyls per line, and the first line's a hyphenated nonsense word, the second line's the proper name. For instance, "Higgledy piggledy,/ Benjamin Harrison,/ Twenty-third president/ was, and, as such,/ Served between Clevelands and/ Save for this trivial/ Idiosyncrasy,/ Didn't do much."

The clerihew, however, is a "humorous, pseudo-biographical verse of four lines of uneven length, with the rhyming scheme AABB, and the first line containing the name of the subject." We'll celebrate National Poetry Month and close with this clerihewical tribute to pronouns by W.H. Auden: "Sir Henry Rider Haggard/ Was completely staggered/ When his bride-to-be/ Announced "I am 'She'!"

Language Maps, Persistent Words, and Stereotypical Incomprehensibility

....

"**25** Maps That Explain the English Language" is a marvelously informative way to look at our Mother Tongue. It's difficult to convey graphic maps in print, so a visit to the source, **www.Vox.com**, is worth the effort. Any description I attempt of Minna Sundberg's gorgeous "Comprehensive Overlook of the Nordic Languages in Their Old World Families" is doomed to failure. However, the article incudes excellent textual information, too. For example, the maps cover the major evolutionary epochs in the development of; some that you might know readily, like "The Anglo-Saxon Migration," but others, such as "Danelaw" and "The Great Vowel Shift", are less familiar.

It was news to me that we still use 4,500 Anglo-Saxon words today, such as "day," "year," "think," "kiss," and 'love," and these amount to about 1 percent of the modern English vocabulary. Danelaw is the period of the Denmark-based Viking invasion of Britain under lamentably-nicknamed Ivar the Boneless, beginning in the 800s. Norse terms from this period that remain in our vocabulary include "law," "murder," and the pronouns "they," "them," and "their." But while "leg" and "husband" are Norse, "arm" and "wife" are Anglo-Saxon. William and the Normans arrived in 1066, infusing all sorts of fancy French words into our ever-evolving tongue. So while the coarse Anglo-Saxons "sweated," the Normans "perspired."

The Great Vowel Shift encompasses the striking evolution in pronunciation that occurred for unknown reasons between 1400, the age of Chaucer's Middle English, and 1700, the time of DeFoe and Swift. In essence, English-speakers began pronouncing long vowels higher up in their mouths than their predecessors. The example given on the Geoffrey Chaucer Page on the **Harvard. edu** website, is "Middle English 'long e' in Chaucer's 'sheep' had the value of Latin 'e' (and sounded like Modern English 'shape')". Not all words with those vowels shifted, and words with "ea" usually kept their old pronunciations. But you can blame the GVS for "steak" and "streak" not rhyming, and for "mice" no longer being pronounced "meese."

It's no wonder that Chinese speakers find English as difficult to grasp as English and Spanish speakers find Greek. Shakespeare wrote "It's all Greek to me" in Julius Caesar, and some Spanish etymologists say that "gringo" comes from "hablar en griego," meaning "to speak in Greek, or unintelligibly." A recent **WashingtonPost.com** article on this said, "The phrase actually comes from a Medieval Latin proverb, 'Graecum est; non potest legi,' meaning 'It is Greek; it cannot be read.'"

The Language Log page on the **UPenn.edu** website provides a "Directed Graph of Stereotypical Incomprehensibility," a title that ought to discourage most Chinese readers. It's a flow-chart with circles showing the 36 major languages with arrows pointing out which languages are incomprehensible to the speakers of others. Arabic speakers, for instance, also find Greek enigmatic, and also Hindi. Persians find Turkish cryptic, while the Turks find French trying, French find Chinese mystifying, the Chinese find English puzzling; we also find Dutch troubling, the Dutch find Latin perplexing, and Latin speakers say the same about Greek.

Nonetheless, a study released by Northwestern University last fall found that "Speaking more than one language is good for the brain" since "bilingual speakers process information more efficiently and more easily... The benefits occur because the bilingual brain is constantly activating both languages and choosing which language to use and which to ignore... When the brain is constantly exercised in this way, it doesn't have to work as hard to perform cognitive tasks, the researchers found." This is scary news for those of us who find all other languages challenging, because our sad brains, for better or worse, are simply wired differently. Fortunately, our public library has a wealth of language-learning aides, including the wonderful Mango database, a slew of books and CDs, as well as foreign-language movies.

Many of our greatest wordsmiths, like Abraham Lincoln, Mark Twain, and Winston Churchill, often drew on the Anglo-Saxon part of our vocabulary. The president's friend William Jayne wrote, "Mr. Lincoln's language and style were Anglo-Saxon; he was not a classical scholar, his words were English pure and clear... The common people understood his arguments."

Or as Mark Twain put it, "Let us make a special effort to stop communicating with each other, so we can have some conversation."

Guys Ropes, Guy Fawlkes, and Guys Read

....

Curious about the origin of the term "guy," as in "Guys Read Program," I opened my trusty 1937 edition of H.L. Mencken's great 1936 classic study of American words, "American Language." Years ago I learned that this book offers almost unlimited browsing ecstasy for those interested in where our language comes from. This time an extra measure of interest was meted out in the form of an old 1950s-era clipping, "Have Ya Got a Geet for the Dil-Ya-Bla?," that was tucked into a previously unexamined series of the back pages of my personal copy of "American Language." "In addition to its influences on the 'music' and clothing worlds, whether you want to believe it or not, Bebop has also made its contributions to the English Language," the article begins. "If you ever get caught between two Bebopers, these are some of the words they may use: Let's scarf, Daddy-O (Let's eat, friend), Oop-pop-a-sa, nab! (Hello, cop!), Pay some dues on the Hollywood eyes (Spend some money on that pretty girl), and Lu cu pu, lop-pow (Good night, every-thing's OK)."

None of those hepcat phrases lasted long, and only a couple of the Bebop terms endured to modern times, and then in modified form: "gig" (defined then as a job for one night only), and "turn on" (smoke a cigarette). In comparison, "guy" has done quite well. According to Mencken, "A 'guy' in England is a ridiculous figure, and thus the word is opprobrious; in the United States the word is hardly more than an amiable synonym for fellow. The English 'guy' owes its origin to the effigies of Guy Fawlkes, leader of the Gunpowder Plot of 1605...the American word seems to be derived from the 'guy-rope' of a circus tent, and first appeared in the complimentary form of 'head-guy.'"

Mencken, who had no advanced education, referred to his "American Language" as "a gaudy piece of buncombe, rather neatly done." However, the book was also "the first attempt since Noah Webster's at an overview of the national language," as a critic noted in "The Wilson Quarterly." Mencken wrote than "Buncombe" was the name of a North Carolina county whose Congressman insisted on speaking dully and to no effect on so many legislative issues that it came to mean "empty talk." It was adopted in England as "bunkum," and then "the American clipped form 'bunk' arose toward the end of the World War," and "the verb 'debunk' followed ten years later."

Mencken scorned academia almost as much as the rude "yokelry," a term he coined, who created and adopted new Americanisms willy-nilly. Shortly after his book's publication, he wrote to a friend, "The truth is that the academic idiots are taking it all very seriously, greatly to my joy." He reveled in his cynicism, but in fact he'd created a significant and entertaining addition to American literature.

Mencken did most of his research for the book during the World War I era. He was as proud of his German ancestry as he was of Baltimore, his hometown. He was also suspicious of the British propaganda machine and wrote about it in no uncertain terms. When war fever was aroused in America, Mencken's popularity as the country's leading journalist plummeted, so he retreated into etymological research, the results of which is on your library's shelves.

There you can also check out most of the books featured by the local Guys Read program. The more than sixty titles were chosen to appeal to fourth grade boys, because that's when most boys stop reading for pleasure. The program's designed to show them that some books are lots of fun. We created the Guys Read program right here in Fairbanks eleven years ago as a way to attract non-library-using families to come in and discover the many new wonders public libraries offer. But it was soon apparent that the program's biggest effect was inspiring boys to read for fun.

You're probably familiar with our local library's many splendid offerings, like the telephone reference service. As they say if you want a hundred million answers to a question, ask Mr. Google, but if you want the correct answer, call a librarian. You can speak to a real live one by dialing 459-1046. For example, they'll happily look up word and phrase origins, such as Bebop's "geet for the dil-ya-bla" once meant "money for the telephone."

Ironic Mindfulness, Forgetting to Remember, and the Helpfulness of Samuel Smiles

....

The world's rich in irony when you're inclined to look for it. Take the word "mindfulness," for example. A recent KUAC radio program featured a book about being mindful while eating, which reminded me that mindfulness was something I intended to write about, along with new ways I've read about recently that improve and reduce one's memory. "Mindfulness" was the focus of Virginia Heffernan's NY Times article last month in which she said the term may be new-sounding and trendy, but compared with other neologisms, like "affluence," "selfie," and "impactful," in which "notes of cynicism and cutesiness come through, "mindfulness" is a useful addition to the lexicon, and, moreover, it's durable.

"It looks like nothing more than the noun form of 'mindful,' but 'mindfulness' has more exotic origins. In the late 19th century…a British magistrate in Ceylon (now Sri Lanka), with the formidable name of Thomas William Rhys Davids, found himself charged with adjudicating Buddhist ecclesiastical disputes. He set out to learn Pali, a Middle Indo-Aryan tongue and the liturgical language of Theravada, an early branch of Buddhism. In 1881, he thus pulled out 'mindfulness'—a synonym for 'attention' from 1530—as an approximate translation of the Buddhist concept 'sati'… Sati, which Buddhists consider the first of seven factors of enlightenment, means, more nearly, 'memory of the present.'"

Flash forward a century, and "Jon Kabat-Zinn, a molecular biologist in New England and a longtime meditator in the Zen Buddhist tradition, saw in Rhys Davids' term a chance to scrub meditation of its religious origins. Kabat-Zinn believed that many of the secular people who could most benefit from meditation were being turned off by the whiffs of reincarnation and other religious esoterica that clung to it." His definition, "the awareness that arises through paying attention on purpose to the present moment non-judgmentally," seems to have stuck.

Whether I'll remember to meditate's another question. So I read "Closing Your Eyes Boosts Memory Recall," a **ScienceDaily. com** article from last January, with special interest. It described a University of Surrey (UK) study that "found evidence that eyewitnesses to crimes remember more accurate details when they close their eyes." The researchers also learned that "building rapport with witnesses also helped them to remember more... Although closing your eyes to remember seems to work whether or not rapport has been built beforehand, our results show that building rapport makes witnesses more at ease with closing their eyes."

But what if you want to forget? A May 2014 Smithsonian Magazine article by Richard Coniff stated that "the best way to forget an alarming memory, oddly, is to remember it first." Sufferers from post-traumatic stress disorder "are often asked by therapists to recall the incident that taught them the fear in the first place. Stirring up a memory makes it a little unstable, and for a window of perhaps three hours, it's possible to modify it before it settles down again, or 'reconsolidates,' in the brain. Reliving traumatic moments over and over in safe conditions can help a person unlearn the automatic feeling of alarm."

This apparently works better with recent traumas than older ones. However, a new drug, histone deacetylase inhibitors, or HDAC, "boost the activity of genes in ways that help brain cells form new connections... The HDAC inhibitors alone had no effect, but drugs and therapy together seemed to open up and reconnect the neurons where long-term memory had been locked away." Meanwhile, University of Alabama at Birmingham researchers are exploring how the brain remembers pleasurable experiences, especially addictive ones.

Our public library's loaded with self-help books intended to help improve memory, eating healthy, getting exercise, being organized, leading others, etc. Self-help books have been popular since Samuel Smiles invented them in 1859. Although already a successful journalist, Smiles' book, "Self-Help," sold over 250,000 copies and "brought Smiles to celebrity status; almost overnight he became a leading pundit and much-consulted guru."

Ironically, Smiles had great hopes for his follow-up book, titled "Conduct," but his publisher, John Murray, refused to help. After Smile's death a copy was found in his desk, but Murray had it destroyed. "The reason why so little is done," as Samuel Smiles said, "is generally because so little is attempted."

Babel's Library, People's Horsebreeder, and Organelles

Back when Larry McMurtry, the author of "Lonesome Dove"—perhaps the Great American Western Novel—was 18 and first entered the Rice University library, he felt that "The whole of the world's literature lay before me unread, a country as vast, as promising, and, so far, as I knew, as trackless as the West must have seemed to the first white men who looked upon it." Had McMurtry considered a moment, he might have realized that the West was filled with the tracks of pre-pioneers, and that librarians had long before begun tracking, arranging, and organizing the world of literature, and still do. Successful libraries balance the need to organize and protect their collections with providing open-hearted assistance to end-users.

Compare our finely-tuned local libraries with that imagined by Jorge Luis Borges in his dystopian short story, "Library of Babel." The **OpenCulture.com** website quotes Borges' vision of the ultimate library. It comprised "a huge number of connected hexagonal rooms lined by bookshelves. 'Each shelf contains thirty-five books of uniform format; each book is of four hundred and ten pages; each page, of forty lines, each line, of some eighty letters which are black in color.' Each book contains a different combination of letters, and in total they contain all possible combinations of letters, with the result that the Library as a whole contains 'Everything: the minutely detailed history of the future, the archangels' autobiographies, the faithful catalogues of the Library, thousands and thousands of false catalogues...'"

How pleasurable would being in such a library actually be? Naturally, the Internet knows. It includes **LibraryofBabel.info**, designed by Jonathan Basile, which uses an algorithm that produces digital books in the format described by Borges. **LibraryofBabel. info** presently "contains all possible pages of 3200 characters, about 10^{4677} (1 followed by 4677 zeroes) books." Visitors can browse these "books" and report any unusual sightings to the website's forum. Sound fun? A typical "book" is titled "rf,xwjofl vfpvr," and begins, ".hgudygonfgvnuvdhlsfoyck,ulxvdlvnvn jswabkegkbenojxigx."

Speaking of strange titles, a **TheGuardian.com** article from last April was titled "You Call Yourself the People's Horse Breeder? The Strange Titles World Rulers Give Themselves." It focused on "Turkmenistan's authoritarian president, Gurbanguly Berdymukhamedov (aka the headline-writer's friend)," who recently gave himself the horse-breeder title. His predecessor "renamed the months of the year after himself and members of his family. Compared to such grandiosity, the People's Horsebreeder, who happens to be a former dentist has so far proved to be the soul of restraint."

The Oxford English Dictionary harbored little restraint when it announced last month, according to the Sunday Times, that it will henceforth include not only Mr., Mrs., Miss, and Ms., but also "the gender-neutral honorific, Mx.—pronounced 'mix'—to represent transgender people and people who don't want to be identified by gender." Pointing out that Ms. was once new, too, NY Times columnist Ben Zimmer found that a letter to the editor of a Springfield, Massachusetts newspaper dated November 10, 1901 noted "to call a maiden Mrs. is only a shade worse than to insult a matron with the inferior title Miss. Yet it is not always easy to know the facts."

Adopting "Ms." was discussed off and on until 1961, when "22-year-old civil rights worker Sheila Michaels saw it on a piece of her roommate's mail and began a crusade in public for its use. Gloria Steinem heard her in a radio interview passionately arguing for the feminist honorific. The first issue of Steinem's 'Ms.' appeared in December 1971, and the rest is history."

Honorifics help keep us categorized, but how do your individual cells organize themselves? Apparently ribbons of spinning proteins help, according to a study by John Hopkins reported in **ScienceDaily.com**. "Each cell is a busy warehouse of activity. To keep things orderly, protein workers are 'assigned' specific area of the cell where other workers are collaborating on the same project. Most of the project areas, or organelles, in the cell are cordoned off by flexible membranes that let things in and out on an as-needed basis." The organelles that handle RNA—the blueprints for proteins used to build cells—were thought to float about like oil droplets in water. Researchers used "state-of-the-art microscopes" to see that RNA organelles are actually inside "irregularly-shaped protein cages" that stabilize them, demonstrating once again that there's usually method to the organizational madness.

Vampires, Toilet Etiquette,
and the Queen of Sheba

....

W e're forest dwellers, and our annual war with the carpenter
ants has begun. This year's invasion put me in mind of an
old article I'd clipped for my file of possibilities I collect for columns
Digging it out revealed an intriguing array of unread trivial tidbits
that didn't make the cut for earlier columns, as well as an interesting article about vampire ants. Posted in 2012 on **YourWildlife.org**
under "Halloween Horrors in the Front Yard," the latter describes
vampire ants as "specialist predators on soil anthropods, specifically
centipedes, that also sometimes feed on the body fluids of their own
larvae…they drink the blood of their babies." It later explained that
the ants do this when food is scarce, and doing it doesn't actually
kill their babies since it's "type of vampirism called 'nondestructive
cannibalism' [that] does not harm the young."

The very next article, from Discover Magazine, described the
curious Chinese soft-shelled turtle that "looks like someone glued the
snout of a pig onto the face of a fish." It lives in saltwater marshes and
can't drink enough of the briny water to utilize its kidneys without
toxic levels of salts accruing. So it "gets rid of most of its urea through
its mouth instead of its kidneys, via gill-like studs in its mouth. It can
breath and get rid of waste through the same structures."

A news story along those lines was forwarded by a retired
librarian from Kodiak who'd attended one of my "Potty Talk"

lectures on public library restroom security at the Alaska Library Association conferences. The article, titled "Over or Under: Toilet Paper Debate," included Seth Wheeler's 1891 patent for toilet paper that states "My invention consists of a roll of wrapping paper with perforations on the line of the division between one sheet and the next, so as to be easily torn apart." Attached is his diagram clearly showing the paper unspooling over the top of the roll, not below. So now everyone on either side of the over-under debate can move on. A related article dealt with the "Aryan Code of Toilets." In 1500 BCE Aryan scribes compiled of list of rules governing everything to do with toiletry. Typical of the strictures is one requiring that before relieving oneself, one must roll a sacred thread into a ball and put it on the right ear, and if one's head isn't covered, the other end of the thread should be placed over the left ear.

There were library-related articles in the column-fodder file, too. One described how Suetonius, my favorite classical author who died in 130 CE, and the author of the wonderfully ribald history "The Twelve Caesars," was also a librarian, being named director of the Library at Alexandria by the Emperor Tiberius. Tiberius loved libraries and had a large one built beside his palace. He called its director Procurator Bibliothecarum, which I'd like on my resume.

Another file item, an excerpt from "The Library: An Illustrated History," described the libraries in the Kingdom of Aksum. Not only was this city-state home for the Queen of Sheba and the reputed current location of the ancient Ark of the Covenant, Aksum's rulers spoke and read Greek and "put great store in written documents and in libraries to keep them." Around 350 CE Aksum was "the first significant empire to accept Christianity" when Frumentius, a Greek Phoenician slave-teacher converted Aksum's King Ezana. Although declining three hundred years later, "Aksum would be more commonly referred to by medieval writers as Ethiopia, [and] remembered as an educated, literate society that cherished libraries."

There's more to libraries than hoarding information. The Aksumites, like many ancients, weren't eager to share their books.

A Chinese proverb in the column file spoke to this: "a book tightly shut is but a block of paper." Some chocolate will help you remember that. "A Bite to Remember? Chocolate Is Shown to Aid Memory," a NY Times article from 2014, said that the flavanol chemical compound found in chocolate "improved blood circulation, heart health, and memory in mice, snails, and humans."

I can't resist collecting such fascinating factoids and agree with Harvard business professor Joseph Badaracco, who said "In today's environment, hoarding knowledge ultimately erodes your power. If you know something important, the way to get power is by actually sharing it."

Pronouncing, Murals, and Building Vocabularies

"Pronunciation Errors That Changed Modern English" was a fascinating article from **TheGuardian.com** posted by David Shariatmadari in 2014. He noted that, "The 20-volume Oxford English Dictionary (OED) lists 171,476 words as being in common use. But the average person's vocabulary is tens of thousand smaller, and the number of words they use every day smaller still. There are bound to be things we've read or are vaguely familiar with, but not able to pronounce as we are supposed to."

This sometimes leads to the letters in words shifting over time. For example, there's "orrebracketing," which occurs when the pronounciation of "a" or "an" before a word results in words that used to be spelled "nadder," "numpire," and "napron" to be misheard and mispronounced so often they evolved into "adder," "umpire," and "apron." Occasionally letters in words move around, and that's how "waps," "brids," and "hros" became "wasps," "birds," and "horse." Linguists call that "metathesis." It's "epenthesis" when our mouths find adding an extra letter more comfortable, like turning "thuner" into "thunder" and "emty" into "empty."

Then there are "syncopes," words that have lost the sounds of some of their letters, such as "Christmas," with its silent "t," and "Woden's day" morphing into "Wednesday." Shariatmadari wrote that "[b]orrowing from other languages can give rise to an entirely understandable and utterly charming kind of mistake" known as "folk etyomology. With little or no knowledge of the foreign tongue, we go for an approximation that makes some kind of sense in terms of sound and meaning." That's how the French term for lobster, "ecrevisse," became "crayfish, the Algonquin word for "red," "muscascus," became "muskrat," and the Old French word for "woman," "femelle," became "female."

Shariatmadari's article links to a BBC article about research conducted by Global Language Monitor (GLM), an Austin, Texas company, showing that on average most native English speakers know 50,000 of the estimated one-to-two million words in our language. Those with college educations average about 75,000, and those without college backgrounds know about 35,000. These are gross generalizations, however, and a person's active reading is a better predictor of vocabulary strength than education levels. Allan Simmons, the 2013 British Scrabble champion, said he "can recognize around 100,000 of the 160,000 words of nine letters or under included on the Scrabble list. Guess what, Allan? GLM says a new English word's created every 98 minutes, and the Scrabble overseers added 6,500 new words last month. Many of these, like "ridic" (ridiculous) and "wahh" (wailing) come from the linguistic evolution generated by technology and social media. Now "Bezzy" (best friend) scores 18 points, for instance, and emoji (expressive digital icon) gets 14.

Last week's News Miner "Brushing Up Fairbanks" article about public art, described some of the new local outdoor murals. However, the term "murals" includes more than wall paintings. "Mural" comes from "murus," Latin for "wall." According to the **DailyWritingTips.com** blog, the OED "'mural' in the context of painting is an American coinage from 1908. In earlier British usage, a mural was 'a fruit tree grown against and fastened to a wall. In US urban settings, mural is used in its customary sense, but recently it has come to be used of paintings made on sidewalks, on streets, and even on such things as benches."

A marvelous mural, the best in town in my opinion, resides in Noel Wien Library. Titled "The Alaska Fairy Tale," it was created by Bill Berry in 1979, and completed after Berry's death by Trina Schart Hyman. The mural hangs in the William Berry Room, the children's area named after that great wildlife artist, and it's inspired thousands of young Alaskans attending the public library's Summer Reading Program activities to extend the dreams of childhood into their adult lives through the magic of reading.

"Reading should not be presented to children as a chore, a duty. It should be offered as a gift," as Kate DiCamillo wisely wrote. Taking the kid in your life to the library makes for some marvelous lifelong summertime memories for you both. Besides, children who read make for better Scrabble competition, and, like Fran Lebowitz noted, "Children are the most desirable opponents at Scrabble as they are both easy to beat and fun to cheat."

Little Words, Ngrams, and Smiley Faces

....

"It's the little details that are vital," according to legendary UCLA basketball coach John Wooden, who added, "Little things make big things happen." For example, take the little words "a" and "an." The Online Etymology Dictionary notes that sometimes words beginning with "n," like "nickname" and "newt," originally began with vowels. For example, until the mid-1400s "nickname" was "ekename," meaning "an additional name," with "eke" coming from the Old English "eaca" ("an increase"). For easier pronunciation English employs the articles "a" before words beginning with consonants and "an" before those starting with vowels. Spelling more closely resembled spoken English in those preliterate days, and "idiot," "island," and "ox" were soon temporarily being spelled "nidiot," "neilond," and "nox."

But what about words starting with an aspirate "h" which sounds like a vowel? A recent **DailyWritingTips.com** posting by Maeve Maddox addressed this, stating that people saying "an historic event" instead of "a historic" are often considered snooty, self-conscious, pompous, and affected. The major opinion setters, such as "The Chicago Manual of Style" and "The Penguin Writer's Manual," agree that "a historic" is correct in modern usage. But Google's Ngram Reader proves it hasn't always been so.

The Ngram Viewer is a website where usage of a word or phrase between 1800 and 2012 can be compared year-by-year. The Google Books project has digitized millions of books and other written sources, and the Ngram program draws on this enormous database. Maddox wrote that doing a comparative search of "a historical" and "an historical" showed that "[i]n 1800, 'a historic' barely shows... In 1869, 'a historic' is neck and neck with 'an historic.' The two travel along fairly close together until the First World War when 'an historic' pulls ahead and dominates until 1938. After that, 'a historic' becomes the clear winner."

"Emoji," defined by Oxford Dictionaries as "small digital images or icons used to express an idea, emotion, etc. in electronic communications," are small words of a kind, too. It began in September 19, 1982 when Scott Fahlman sent a message to the Carnegie Mellon University computer science department with a smiley face made by typing a colon, a hyphen, and a parenthesis, as in ":-)." He was the first to do it on a computer, but the same symbol's been in use at least since the 1800s. For example, "Puck," the British humor magazine, ran a series of similar punctuation-based symbols in March 1881. Today most keyboards insert ☺ automatically after ":-" is typed. Spin-offs abound, such as :-& (tongue-tied), 3:) (devilish), and #-) (partied all night).

The smiley symbol got the name "emoticon" in 1990 when the words "emotion" and "icon" were blended together. Wikipedia states that the emoticon "is a metacommunicative pictorial representation of a facial expression that, in the absence of body language and prosody, serves to draw a receiver's attention to the tenor or temper of a sender's nominal non-verbal communication, changing and improving its interpretation." In other words, they help convey the writer's feelings. "Emoji," which is Japanese for "pictographs," was adopted in 1997 to describe the bevy of emoticons being included in Unicode, the "character encoding standard for computer storage and transmission of the letters, characters, and symbols of most languages and writing systems," that standardize the digitalizing of most of the world alphabets and symbols used for communicating. Today Unicode contains over 700 emoji, including little yellow faces that sweat, snooze, wear sunglasses, look like cats, and many more.

Speaking of small symbols, there's a little-known library-related one worth knowing: "OZ." It has nothing to do with L. Frank Baum and the Emerald City, but could have everything to do with locating a special book. "OZ" on the catalog note means "over-sized" in library lingo. Large coffee-table books are usually gathered in a separate location to prevent their size from forcing some bookshelves to be spaced further apart than required by normally-sized books. Our public libraries keep the OZs at the end of the nonfiction sections where the shelves are further apart.

Keeping 300,000+ items in the right place is a monumental and never-ending task for our local librarians, but their paying careful attention to that little detail enables everyone else to find what they want. As Arthur Conan Doyle said, "the little things are infinitely the most important."

Lazy Men, Ugly Men, and Human Books

....

It's hard to peruse Dorothy Johnson's "Bedside Book of Bastards" without musing ruefully on mankind, specifically the man part. True, some rascally women are included, but most of Johnson's subjects are really bad guys, like the 15th-century French baron Gilles de Rais, who, on one hand, was Joan of Arc's companion in arms, and a serial murderer of scores of children on the other. Most guys aren't in the same league as Attila or the Borgias, but apparently it's mostly a matter of degree.

The recent research is sadly compelling. Take the Washington Post article from last May titled "Study: Men Are Lazy to Their Core," by Christopher Ingraham, who cites University of Maryland research that shows that today's average American woman does 1.7 times as much housework as the average man. Fortunately, "men are simply more slovenly than women, and less averse to filth."

It could be worse; Takanakuy isn't popular here yet. "Takanakuy" means "when the blood is boiling" in the Quechua language of Peru. Peruvian men dress in wild costumes and pair off in rural arenas for a series of fistfights. "The purpose of Takanakuy is to settle grievances built up over the year…in a public forum," according to **BBC.com**. "People of all ages enter the ring, from young children to the elderly, and participation is open to women and men alike… The fights themselves are relatively civil, bearing closer resemblance to martial arts sparring than uninhibited brawls." There are also referees who carry whips.

The fighters wear colorful ski masks while fighting and other symbolic garb, according to Wikipedia. "The main purpose of the ski mask is to conceal the identity of the fighters to prevent tensions and animosities lingering into the next year." There are five traditional characters portrayed by the fighters. The "Majenos" horsemen for example, wear wool riding pants, short jackets, chaps, "and either a dead bird or a deer skull on top of his/her head." The "langostas" are the locusts whose costumes are made out of shiny materials, and they usually carry dead birds to represent the death that locusts caused during the 1940s.

Colorful ski masks might become popular with America's homely men. In "Homely Men Who Misbehave Can't Win for Losing," a recent **ScienceDaily.com** article cites researchers' from Eastern Kentucky University findings that "a woman's view of a man is influenced by how handsome and law-abiding he is." They studied female jurors and users of online dating services and found that "(w) omen tolerate an unattractive man up to a point, but beware if he misbehaves. Then they'll easily shun him… In what is called the 'halo effect,' people warm up to others with positive characteristics, such as handsomeness. The 'devil effect,' or 'negative halo effect,' comes into play when people assume that others possess so-called 'bad' characteristics based on traits such as unattractiveness."

The study found that "transgressing a social norm" counted for more than attractiveness. "Normally women do not feel differently towards a homely man who toes the line." However, if an ugly guy "transgresses the boundaries of right or wrong, a magnified 'double devil effect' comes into play. He is then viewed in an extremely negative light, much more so than would have been the case if he were handsome."

An ugly Peruvian house-husband might make an intriguing human book to check out. "Human Libraries" is a 15-year-old concept in which library patrons are invited to "borrow" people who've agreed to be interviewed to learn more about them. They can be checked out for half- or full hour sessions, and they can be reserved in advance. At the Toronto Public Library, for instance, patrons could choose from a police officer, comedian, cancer survivor, model, "a sex-worker-turned-club-owner, and homeless person. The idea was created by a youth organization in Copenhagen and has spread to 30 countries. Featured human books include police, bikers, gay couples, clowns, writers, and many others.

People come to the library to learn, reflect, and interact. Our public library's resources and services are such that it is indeed The People's University. But with its meetings, gatherings, and information sharing of all sorts, it's also everyone's Community Commons, regardless of their physical beauty.

Love, Mistakes, and Marilyn Monroe

....

So tell me: Who wrote the book of love? You might say it was the 1950s one-hit wonder doo-wop group, the Monotones who did indeed write and record a popular song by that title, but you'd be mistaken. The Monotones were inspired by the Pepsodent commercial jingle that ended with "You'll wonder where the yellow went when you brush your teeth with Pepsodent." And the "boom" in the line, "Tell me, tell me who-doo-doo-doo-doo, (boom): who wrote the book of love," originated with a neighbor kid who kept rhythmically kicking a ball against the wall of the garage the band was rehearsing in.

Some might claim that the courtier Andreas Capellanus, AKA Andrew the Chaplin, wrote the book of love when around 1185 he penned "De Arte Honesti Amandi," or "The Art of Honorable Loving," for the Countess Marie de Champagne. They'd be mistaken, too. According to Andrea Hopkins' "The Book of Courtly Love: the Passionate Code of the Troubadours," Capellanus listed many rules governing proper love, such as "Love that is made public rarely lasts" and "A small supposition compels a lover to suspect his beloved of doing wrong." But Capellanus had predecessors, too.

The Roman poet Ovid wrote the first book of love, or at least, the first best-seller on the topic. His "Ars Amatoria," of "The Art of Love," written in 2 A.D., contains three books. Where the Monotones suggested "In chapter one you love her; you love her with all your heart," Ovid's first book focused on how men can find the right woman. The Monotones' second chapter, "you tell her, you're never-never-never-never-never gonna part," was countered by Ovid's book two: how to keep her. For example, he suggested things like "not forgetting her birthday" and "letting her miss you, but not for too long." And while the Monotones recommend breaking up, but then giving her one more chance, Ovid's third book is aimed at advising women how to keep their men, including "making up in private" after tiffs.

No one's above making occasional mistakes. Experience," as Oscar Wilde pointed out, "is simply the name we give our mistakes." I garnered more experience last week by submitting an old draft of last week's column to the News Miner instead of the corrected and improved version. Perhaps you didn't notice, but to me it seemed glaringly disjointed and error-ridden. You can see the intended version at **HillofBooks.org**, my blog-o-columns where articles previously published in the News Miner live forever, along with explanatory illustrations.

Librarians and journalists make mistakes, too. Washington Post correspondent Michael Rosenwald's recent article in our local newspaper, "Libraries Check Out the Future of Less Paper, More Pixels," looked at how shrinking library budgets are forcing them to buy fewer print books and more digital books. "Libraries have to evolve or die," said the director of a large Maryland public library system. "We're probably the classic example of Darwinism." I don't believe today's libraries are in the same position blacksmiths found themselves when autos were invented. That ignores the enduring popularity of print, and how reading print and digital books are very different experiences.

Deloitte, the international financial consulting firm, predicted earlier this year, "that in 2015 print will represent more than 80 percent of all book sales in dollars worldwide. In the US, the world's largest book market, the figure is lower at just under 80 percent, but the percentage of print is higher in other developed world countries, and even more so in the developing world. A decade on from the launch of the eReader, print still dominates book sales even in markets with high digital device penetration—and print will likely generate the majority of books sales for the foreseeable future. Sales of eBooks have hit a plateau, or seen decelerating growth, in major markets including the US, UK and Canada."

When it comes to the prophesied demise of print, a little more research and less fear-mongering seems applicable. My self-inflicted setbacks always pain me sharply, but librarians saying print's on the way out is short-sighted and ill-informed. I'm sure to screw up again, but as Marilyn Monroe said, "I'm selfish, impatient, and a little insecure. I make mistakes, I'm out of control, and at times hard to handle. But if you can't handle me at my worst, then you sure as hell don't deserve me at my best."

Admiral Wrangell, Word-Lists, and Venery

....

Fishing in Alaska with Outside college buddies can be challenging for a librarian. Many people believe librarians are limitless fonts of all knowledge when they're merely actually trained to know where desired information's likely to be found. So when my pals asked about the Wrangell Mountains' namesake, I immediately turned to Orth's "Dictionary of Alaska Place Names," a prime Alaskana reference book. There I learned about Admiral Ferdinand Friedrich Georg Ludwig von Wrangel, beginning with Wikipedia's assertion that "In English texts, 'Wrangel' is sometimes spelled Vrangel, a transliteration from Russian, which more closely represents its pronunciation in German, or 'Wrangell.'"

Wrangell was a Baltic German and an explorer for the Russian government. He governed the Russian Alaska settlements from 1829-1834, and his initiatives there included introducing potatoes for cultivation and encouraging mining and the fur trade. But the achievement that caught my bibliographic eye was Wrangell's "Word-Lists of the Languages of Russian Alaska." Originally an 1839 compilation comparing German, Russian, and Yup'ik expressions, English terms were added to the 2009 online version. Now you can read comparisons like "Comet, Komet, Kometa, and Azbrxhaxmakb" at **www.asna.ca/alaska/research/slovar.pdf.**

A good wordlist is joyful to behold, and they're legion on the Internet, and they're usually absurdly subjective. Take "100 Beautiful Words From the English Language You Need to Use More" from

SoBadSoGood.com. I'll concede some words like "imbroglio (an altercation or complicated situation)," and "desuetude (disuse)," belong on the list. And I noted that "susurrous (whispering)," a particularly favored word of my eldest daughter, made the cut. But how did "brood," "elixer," and "Susquehanna" made that list and not "library," "books," or "reading"?

I'd argue that "venery" should be included. Besides flowing from the tongue, venery includes some interesting connotations. **WorldWideWords.org** says there are two distinct meanings of the term, "the practice or pursuit of sexual pleasure," and "hunting, the sports of the chase." The first goes back to Venus, the Roman goddess of love. The second comes from Latin, too, but in this instance it's "'venerie': to hunt." "Venery refers to hunting game animals such as wild boar, hares, wolves, bears, and especially deer. A close relative to 'venery' is 'venison,' nowadays always meat from a deer but in earlier times the flesh of any hunted animal... The beasts of venery were those that were considered most noble to hunt. There were animals of lower order, too, the beasts of the chase, which included the fox, as well as beasts of the warren, such as the rabbit and the pheasant."

"Venery" also means "collective terms," like "a murder of crows," but even stranger ones exist. There's a "gaze of raccoons," an "intrusion of cockroaches," and a "hover of trout."

Benjamin Franklin wrote about it in his "Autobiography": "Rarely use venery but for health or offspring, never to dullness, weakness, or the injury of your own or another's peace or reputation." That could apply to lechery or hunting in our often confusing language. Naturally, there's a "Top 10 Confused Words in English" list from Maeve Maddox's **DailyWritingTips.com**, including "illicit ('not allowed by law or social conventions)" and "elicit ('to draw out a reply or reaction'), and "imply ('to suggest indirectly')," and "infer ('to draw a conclusion')." My old nemesis "it's" vs "its" is there, too. "Despite the hundreds, perhaps thousands of explanations to be found on the Web regarding the difference between these two spellings," Maeve wrote, "the mistake of writing 'it's' for 'its' remains the most common written error of them all."

Rude word lists abound, too, including a few Samuel Johnson admitted into his iconic 1755 "Dictionary of the English Language." Described by the British National Library as "one of the most famous dictionaries in history," it was an enormous individual accomplishment. With only a few assistants' clerical help, Johnson single-handedly defined 40,000 words in detail and demonstrated them in 140,000 quotations from literature. But he didn't eschew slipping in a few of his favorite racy terms, such as "bum," and "fart."

The real 1765 third edition of Johnson's dictionary can be seen at Noel Wien Library's rare books collection containing gems like "pricklouse (a word of contempt for a tailor)," and "fopdoodle (a fool)." And one for aspiring venelists to fear: "amatorculist (a little insignificant lover)."

Grammar, Justice, and Yahoos

· ·

When grammar rules arise, I enjoy reflecting upon Federal Judge William Wayne Justice, a forward-thinking, progressive jurist who from the early 1940s consistently ruled in favor of civil rights, presiding in East Texas, which generally trended in the other direction. He was nonetheless widely respected within legal circles, his legacy being such that in 2004 the University of Texas Law School, his alma mater, established the William Wayne Justice Center for Public Interest Law.

My father-in-law practiced law in Tyler, Texas, where Judge Justice also resided, for a half-century, and he supported Justice's rulings on civil rights, but generally considered him too liberal. We owned then a registered Weimaraner officially named Wilkomen, but my father-in-law insisted on calling him Willy Wayne as a gentle poke at the judge's ancestry. However, my father-in-law's disgust with our grammar was in dead earnest when we instructed Willy to "lay down," since "lie down" is correct. "Lay," as in "put something or someone down carefully," dates to the late 800s CE, while "lie," as in "to recline," is from around 1010, and we've apparently been getting them mixed up ever since. According to **DailyWritingTips.com's** Maeve Maddox, "The most usual error is to use 'lay' intransitively," as in "Lay down, Willy! "[B]ut some poor conscientious souls, aware that 'lay' is often the wrong choice, are falling into the error of using 'lie' transitively," as in "Lie Willy on the bed."

Maddox says "I've become partially inured to the intransitive use of 'lay'... The alarm clangs only when I observe its use by teachers, broadcast journalists, advertisers, doctors, lawyers, and anyone else whose occupation requires the use of English for public communication." All well and good, but what about last month's article on JSTOR/Daily, ("where news meets its scholarly match"), titled, "Dear Pedants: Your Fave Grammar Rule Is Probably Fake"?

First of all, a "pedant" is not jewelry; it's "a person who gives too much importance to details and formal rules, especially of grammar," according to the Macmillan Dictionary. For example, the forbidden splitting of infinitives and ending sentences with prepositions, like most of their ilk, originated in the Victorian era and "were entirely dreamt up in an age of moral prescriptivism, reflecting nothing of historical or literary usage," but were intended "to encourage the poor English language to be more like an entirely different (and entirely dead) language, namely Latin... The English language didn't change to make those rules obsolete; they were simply fictional from the start."

When it comes to splitting infinitives, most everyone's done it before and after the Victorian crypto-Latin rule-makers unilaterally laid down their grammar laws, because our language's nuances require that sort of flexibility. As the article notes, the phrase "You really have to watch him" hasn't the same connotations as "You have to really watch him."

That brings us to "yahoos." The American Heritage Dictionary defines "yahoo" as "a rude, noisy, or violent person." It was coined by Jonathan Swift for "Gulliver's Travels," in which Gulliver meets Yahoos while traveling to various fanciful lands. Since its 1726 publication, scholars have debated the hidden meanings of the mysterious words Swift attributed to the languages of the tiny Lilliputians, the giant Bobdingnags, and the Houyhnhnm, the intelligent horses "tended by deformed savages known as Yahoos." According to **TheGuardian.com**, University of Houston professor Irving Rothman has broken Swift's code, tracing many of the words back to the opposite meanings of Hebrew terms. "Yahoo," Rothman proposes, was a play on YHWH, the Hebrew word for god, which is pronounced "Yahway." Swift's point was that the Yahoos were the natural opposite of everything divine, but apparently the creators of the Yahoo search engine in 1994 weren't paying attention.

Ignoring things is a human trait. For example, most of us insist on calling the onset of night time "sunset," when it's actually the Earth that's doing the moving, not the sun. But ignoring grammar rules is sometimes okay. I just started re-reading my favorite author, Patrick O'Brian, while listening to the audio version from the public library. In O'Brian's novel "Master and Commander," an officer gave dictation lessons to young midshipmen, telling them to "Take those pens and these sheets of paper, and pass him yonder book, which would answer admirably for them to be read to out of from." Reading aloud to youngsters, now that's fun writing; no lie.

Poor Judgment, Nasty Metaphors, and Intolerance

. . . .

Let's consider "visa" and "vis-a-vis." According to the Inline Etymology Dictionary, the word "visa" comes from the Latin "charta visa," which literally means "paper that has been seen." Many thousands of people from Africa and the Middle East currently stranded in Hungary sure wish they had one. The flexible term "vis-à-vis" literally means "face-to-face" when used as an adverb. "Vis-à-vis" can be used as a noun meaning "a political or diplomatic counterpart," and in "corporate speak" it means "regarding, with respect, to." But it comes from "vis," which is Old French for "face."

This came to mind after reading about a Hungarian camerawoman working for **444.hu**, a Hungarian news site "associated with Hungary's far-right Jobbik party," according to the NY Times. She was videotaped as she intentionally tripped up a foreign refugee who was carrying a child while fleeing from the police in a Hungarian "relocation camp." Her act's been widely condemned, but it beggared my assumption that people generally act more civilly when directly facing someone they don't agree with.

"Swarms, Floods, and Marauders: The Toxic Metaphors of the Migration Debate," a recent article from **TheGuardian.com** by David Shariatmadari, looked at the metaphors being used in Britain to describe the refugee crisis facing Europe. Prime Minister Cameron "spoke of a swarm of people coming across the Mediterranean," his foreign secretary called them "marauders," and "even the BBC used 'flood' and 'stream' as verbs to describe the movement of people north out of Italy.'

Macmillan Dictionary describes "metaphor as "a word or phrase that means one thing and is used for referring to another thing in order to emphasize their similar qualities." George Lakoff's "Metaphors We Live By" is a classic on the subject, and it's in our public library's collection. Lakoff "shows just how deeply embedded figures of speech are in our language...they represent fixed ideas that are ultimately just one way of looking at the world." Shariatmadari's article cited a host of our culture's ingrained metaphors, such as "Good Is Up, Bad Is Down" (as in "We hit a peak last year, but it's been downhill ever since"), and "Ideas Are Food" ("Don't spoonfeed your students"). The "swarm" and marauder" metaphors Cameron and his minister employed essentially said "Migrants Are Insects" and "Migrants Are An Invading Army." "When set out so starkly," Shariatmadari wrote, "it's clear that these metaphors are way over the top. Not to mention dehumanizing, ridiculously simplistic, and pitched at around the intellectual level of a dark-ages Anglo Saxon."

"Metaphors," as Richard Dawkins pointed out, "are fine if they aid understanding, but sometimes they get in the way." That's worth keeping in mind, considering the vitriolic tenor of our country's incessant political campaigning, especially on the topic of migrants. Another recent Guardian article noted that with 41 million native Spanish speakers, "the United States is now the world's second largest Spanish-speaking country after Mexico." Some jingoists fear this means that English will soon be surpassed by Spanish. Experts like Brooking Institute demographer William Frey pooh-pooh that notion since "the enthusiasm second- and third-generation Latinos have for English will act as a brake." English is the world language of computers and commerce, so as Frey, states, "English will obviously be the dominant language," especially in the U.S.

It's worth recalling that back in 1900 millions of Americans spoke German. By way of comparison, there were 17,194 English newspapers then and 613 German language ones, with Scandinavian papers coming in third with 115. During World War I anti-German hysteria mounted, and in many states teaching German was made illegal, German music couldn't be performed even privately, and even speaking German was forbidden. Similar sentiments are echoed in today's political rhetoric.

Curmudgeon, essayist, and wordsmith H.L. Mencken, whose parents were both first-generation German immigrants, was proud of his German extraction. He was educated in German-oriented schools in Baltimore, where as a man he frequented German bars. Nonetheless, Mencken became the greatest authority on the history of American English. It's amazing what open and curious minds can achieve, and that's just who our public libraries are meant for. No visas are required. As Lady Bird Johnson pointed out, "no place in any community is so totally democratic as the town library. The only entrance requirement is interest."

Pollution, Holophrasm, and Cekoslovakyalilastiramadiklarimizdanmissiniz

People who look for them often find that new, amusing, and useful words seem to pullulate. **A.Word.A.Day**, that fount of fascinating terms, recently said "pullulate" means "to sprout or breed, to swarm or teem, to increase rapidly." Sure enough, an interesting term was soon encountered: "holophrasm." Words like "holophrasm" are worth rolling about one's mind and supposing what it means, and coming up with potential definitions before learning the true meaning. An immediate red flag was that **OneLook.com**, the authoritative dictionary database, had no definitions for "holophrasm" in it's 1,000-plus dictionary database. However, it cited the **OxfordDictionaries.com** definition of "holophrasis" as, "the expression of a whole phrase in a single word, for example 'howdy' for 'how do you do.'"

There is such a thing as too much verbal pullulation, as most serious students can attest. Like librarians, good researchers cite in their footnotes the sources of information that helped them reach their findings. Many times those sources have long, drawn-out titles, and when the researcher has to footnote the same ones repeatedly, it's beneficial to all concerned to instead use "ibid," an abbreviation of the Latin word "ibidem," which means "in the same place." "Ibid," as Maeve Maddox's **DailyWritingTips.com**, another worthy word site, puts it, "usually refers to a single work cited in the note immediately preceding."

In the ibid spirit, let's revisit several sources of information used in this column recently. Since de-bunking the "print-book-is-dead" myth, it's imperative to share "The Plot Twist: E-Book Sales Slip, and Print Is Far From Dead," a NY Times article from last week by Alexandra Alters that noted that "E-book sales fell by 10 percent in the first five months of this year... The portion of people who read books primarily on e-readers fell to 32 percent in the first quarter of 2015, from 60 percent in 2012, a Nielsen survey showed." A few years ago there was talk about the rising popularity of e-books bringing about the imminent demise of print books, but that pig-headed theory ignored some important factors. For instance, an overwhelming amount of research has proven it's harder to physically read and recall what's been read on a scrolling screen than it is for printed text.

Noah Webster's Blue-Backed Speller also needs another mention. Webster utilized short moralistic practice essays in his spellers' "Easy Standard of Pronunciation" section that are presented in a question-and-answer format. "Of Mercy," for example, begins, "Q. What is mercy? A. It is tenderness of the heart. Q. What are the advantages of this virtue? A. The exercise of it tends to diffuse happiness and lessen the evils of life."

"Of Generosity" begins "Q. What is generosity? A. It is the act of kindness performed for another which strict justice does not demand." That resonated after reading the international legal definition of migrants versus refugees. A "migrant," according to Maddox, "chooses to leave home, but a refugee is forced to seek a place of safety elsewhere." Moreover, "[a]s defined by international law, a 'refugee' is a person who has fled a country to escape war or persecution and can prove it." In other words, without ironclad proof, or if you're fleeing things like poverty or natural disasters, there's no legal sanctuary.

It's awful to have no home. During the breakup of Czechoslovakia, Turks living there were told "Cekoslovakyalila-stiramadiklarimizdanmissiniz," which means "you are reportedly

one of those that we could not make Czechoslovakian." They had
to leave and become illegal refugees.

People in at least one refugee camp will find solace at a library,
though. The tent city outside Calais, France known as "the Jungle"
is "a temporary home for several thousand people, most of whom
have fled East Africa or the Middle East." The camp is near the
"Chunnel," the tunnel between France and Britain, where many of
the refugees hope to go. A September NY Times article by Pamela
Druckerman described a British volunteer named Mary Jones who
has established "a makeshift library...made out of wooden planks
and plastic sheeting with a corrugated metal roof" called "Jungle
Books."

Jungle Books has few resources and contains only a few hundred
cast-off books, but Druckerman noted "that the library is mostly
just a calm place for people to digest what's happened, and mull
what to do next." Having a generous, merciful place to safely be
and consider is a mission worthy of any library.

Irresistible Change, Ain't's Onus, and Catalog Cards

....

"**C**hange," as Benjamin Disraeli pointed out, "is inevitable. Change is constant." Ain't it though? There was a time when "ain't" was considered quite proper grammar. The American Heritage Dictionary remains my favorite, in part because of its marvelous "Usage Notes" for some of the more intriguing terms. In this instance, it read, "Ain't has a long history of controversy. It first appeared in 1778, evolving from an earlier 'an't,' which arose almost a century earlier as a contraction of "'are not' and 'am not.'

"In fact, 'ain't' arose at the tail-end of an era that saw the introduction of a number of our most common contractions, including 'don't' and 'won't.' But while 'don't' and 'won't' eventually became accepted at all levels of speech and writing, 'ain't' was to receive a barrage of criticism in the 19th century for having no set sequence of words from which it can be contracted, and for being a 'vulgarism'...despite all the attempts to ban it, 'ain't' continues to enjoy extensive use in speech."

Nonetheless, sometimes ain't's OK. It's generally acceptable when trying to strike a folksy or colloquial tone, or striving for that. It's something to ponder if you're into online dating. The Grade, a popular app, "ranks the message quality of prospective" online dates." Among other things, it looks for typos and grammar errors in the messages and assigns hopeful Lotharios letter grades from A+ to F.

"What's Really Hot on Dating Sites? Proper Grammar," a recent Wall Street Journal article by Georgia Wells, cited a **Match.com** study that found that apart from personal hygiene, the most important criteria of their subscribers was grammar. "88% of women and 75% of men said they cared about grammar most, putting it ahead of a person's confidence or teeth." For the record, hygiene's importance came in at 96% for women and 91% for men. As Columbia University linguistics professor John McWhorter said, "Grammar snobbery is one of the last permissible prejudices." This partly stems from how language "has become amplified in recent years with increasing informal and colloquial usage," according to Ben Zimmer, the chair of the New Words Committee of the American Dialect Society, who ought to know.

Wells said another reason grammar's so important to dating ads is it "can reflect the level of effort, or lack thereof, that folks put into their bio. 'People use quality of writing as an indication of work ethic,' says Max Lytvyn, co-founder of automated proofreading company Grammarly. Grammarly analyzed spelling errors on dating site eHarmony. A man with two spelling errors on the site was 14% less likely to receive a positive response."

Apparently some women do prefer the phrase "buck naked" over "butt naked." Maeve Maddox, editor of **DailyWritingTips.com**, whose opinions I respect, wrote "I prefer 'buck naked,' because 'butt-naked strikes my ear as excessively vulgar. I cannot, however, argue that one is 'more correct' than the other… Neither, however, has found a place in formal English." Can't say that about "butt-dialing," the kismet event caused by putting one's cell phone in the back pocket, sitting down, and inadvertently auto-dialing someone on your phone's contact list. New words just added to **OxfordDictionaries.com**'s vocabulary include "manspreading—when a man sits with his legs wide apart on public transport encroaching on other seats," "hangry—adjective used to show feelings of anger or irritability as a result of hunger," and, my favorite, "NBD," the three-syllable abbreviation of the three-syllable phrase "no big deal."

The Greek philosopher Heraclitus, "the weeping philosopher," remarked in 500 BCE that "No man ever steps in the same river twice." He lived in Ephesus, home of one of the great classical libraries, which is fitting since this week the last library catalog cards were printed by OCLC, the "world's leading library cooperative," that created the first shared catalog system in 1971. That year OCLC shipped the first of an eventual 1.9 billion printed catalog cards to libraries around the country, including, beginning in 1977, Fairbanks.

Suddenly our local librarians were freed from painstakingly creating the five-to-twenty cards each new book required. Like many seasoned library patrons, I fondly recall the long, thin drawers of golden cards, immediately conveying the wealth of knowledge on that subject held in our library. Then I recall a 3-year-old vomiting into one of my library's catalog drawers back in Texas. Sometimes change ain't so bad.

Fat Ladies, Receipts vs Recipes, and Love Talk

....

"Two Fat Ladies" is a delightful BBC cooking show featuring a couple of chubby upper-crust cooks who cruise around on a sidecar motorcycle visiting famous British sites where they ostentatiously draw upon local and historical "receipts" to prepare culinary feasts. It's part of our public library's excellent DVD collection, but rather than being housed with the movies and television series, it's kept in its main subject area, "Cooking and Cookery," with the related nonfiction books, like most of the nonfiction DVDs. However, the hunt's part of the fun, and the serendipitous aspect of unimpeded browsing through our library's shelves is one of the most obvious ways American public libraries differ from the rest of the world.

Throughout most written history, librarians kept the general population far away from their collections, but access to information has always been prized in this country, and that sentiment's reflected in our libraries' open bookshelves, where the books and other materials are arranged to facilitate people looking around for themselves, and perhaps discovering the unexpected. Serendipity's a powerful ingredient to add to the basic recipe for scratching intellectual itches that begins with "Take one good library, organize it logically, allow people to utilize it well, and keep it in order for the next users."

In 1580s England, "recipe" originally meant "medical prescription," according to the Online Etymological Dictionary. It comes

from the Latin "recipe," which meant "take!," being the imperative singular form of "recipere," "to take." "Receipt" meant the
same as "recipe," but dates from the late-1300s, when Chaucer
used it. It originated from the Latin "receipt," or "he receives."
WorldWideWords.org says the word "recipe," or "take!," was tra-
ditionally the first word in a prescription, heading the list of ingredients. This was often abbreviated to a letter R with a bar through
the leg, a form that still sometimes appears on modern prescription
forms."

The Sumerians, the world's first writers, frequently recorded
medical receipts and incantations, an unsurprising fact since most
of the ancient clay tablets recovered in Mesopotamian ruins are
lists and tallies: accounting rather than literature. The first great
exception was the Epic of Gilgamesh. The online Ancient History
Encyclopedia says "Gilgamesh is the semi-mythic King of Uruk
best known from the Epic of Gilgamesh (written c.2150-1400
BCE)... the oldest piece of epic western literature... Gilgamesh is
widely accepted as the historical 5th king of Uruk whose influence
was so profound that myths of his divine status grew up around his
deeds and finally culminated in 'The Epic of Gilgamesh.'"

This great story was written in cuneiform, an alphabet of wedge-
shaped impressions pressed into soft clay tablets that were then fired
and hardened in kilns. A recent **LiveScience.com** article described
the discovery of a lost tablet from the Gilgamesh epic poem that
describes the hero's adventures in a forest. An Iraqi museum purchased the tablet from a smuggler and translated it within five days.
"The new tablet adds 20 previously unknown lines...filling in some
of the details of how the forest looked and sounded... It is full of
noisy birds and cicadas, and monkeys scream and yell in the trees."

"Phonaesthetics" is the "study of the aesthetic properties of
speech sound, in particular the study of sound sequences." After
encountering the term in a **DailyTelegraph.com** article by Angela
Mollard titled "Pashing. Spooning. Bonk. The Language of Love is
joyless," I suspect that professional phonaestheticians will appreciate

and grapple with elucidating Gilgamesh's jungle sounds. Hopefully Sumerian has better expressions of love that Ms. Mollard's found in English. "Ours may be the third most spoken language in the world," she wrote, "but it's either utilitarian, schmaltzy, or downright crass when it comes to matters of the heart... the nomenclature used to describe not just relationships, but what takes place in them, is dispiritingly ugly."

Mollard notes that other languages abound in graciously loving expressions. "Cavoli riscaldati" is Italian for "reheated cabbage" and means "attempting to fix a failed relationship." "Razbliuto" is Russian for "the lingering fondness you have for one you once loved." And the Germans speak of "kummerspeck," "which literally translates to 'grief bacon' for the emotional overeating that follows heartbreak."

When it comes to our library, give me the Norwegian "forelsket" "the euphoric feeling of falling in love."

Bubbles, Words, and Colors

....

When Saint Augustine said, "This world's a bubble," I think he nailed it. I recently read a **Slate.com** article by Seth Stevenson titled "Bubble Vocabulary: The Words You Almost Know, Sometimes Use, But Are Secretly Unsure Of." He wrote, "We've all experienced moments in which we brush up against the ceilings of our personal lexicons...[w]ords on the edge of your ken, whose definitions or pronunciations turn out to be just out of grasp." It's the common complaint of prolific readers: sometimes unfamiliar words are encountered whose meanings can be generally extracted from the context of the accompanying text.

Take "betimes," for example. It means "before the usual or expected time," according to **OxfordDictionaries.com**, was popular from 1300-1700 CE, and was one of Samuel Pepys' favorite expressions. This I know after reading Pepys' famous diaries of 1660-1669, in which entries often begin with "Up betimes," such as, "Up betimes, about 9 o'clock, waked by a damned noise between a sow gelder and a cow and a dog." After reading similar statements on other days, it appeared "betimes" meant "early," but my uncertainty lingered.

Another "be" word recently engaged my attention: "bespoke." An adulthood of enjoying P.G. Wodehouse's comic tales meant many encounters with the term, "bespoke," but it was many decades on before I confirmed it meant "of goods, especially clothing, made to order." "Bespoke" was recently featured in a graph in the endlessly entertaining Lapham's Quarterly, which is hands-down my favorite magazine. Lapham's is described by Wikipedia as "a literary magazine established in 2007 by former Harper's Magazine editor Lewis H. Lapham. Each issue examines a theme using primary source material from history." **LaphamsQuarterly.org** says "Each issue addresses a topic of current interest and concern—war, religion, money, medicine, nature, crime." Short extracts by great writers and artists throughout history are salted with gorgeous illustrations, pithy quotations, mini-biographies of the writers, and amazing graphs.

The current Lapham's focuses on "Fashion (divided into sections on "Mode, Manners, Mores, and Markets"), and includes the graph "Local Colors," a two-page color wheel composed of unusual hues, their sources, origins, and histories. I was unaware that "Tiffany Blue" was chosen by New York jeweler Charles Tiffany in 1845 for his first catalog, and he liked it so much he trademarked it. "Prussian Blue," created in Berlin in 1705, contains cyanide, which was named after "the Greek 'kyranos, for dark blue." But it was "Egyptian Blue" that sent me to the deep end of the library reference pool.

A discussion with the library reference staff indicated that the topic was promising, and I soon learned from a variety of reputable sources that Egyptian blue is one of the very first artificial pigments used by civilized mankind. The Egyptians adored blue gemstones, especially the then-extremely expensive lapis lazuli and turquoise. Some bright-eyed Egyptian discovered that heating calcium carbonate, copper-infused compounds (filings or malachite), silica sand from granite, and soda produced several shades of turquoise, AKA "Egyptian Blue," that was used to decorate papyrus scrolls and ceramics.

I learned much more about Egyptian Blue's origins in the **AncientOrigins.net** blog, and couldn't help noticing other related and irresistible articles, like "Scota: Mother of Scotland and Daughter of a Pharaoh" and "Exploring the True Origins of Snow

White and the Seven Dwarves." I also wound up reading about another bubble word, "fuller," in an article from the University of Waterloo in Canada titled "Cleverness, Cleanliness, and Urine in Ancient Rome." The heavy wool togas and other garments of the period, being white or light colored, were easily mussed. Roman fullers were "the ancient equivalent of today's dry cleaners...they worked with urine, nitrum, or fuller's earth in laundering. Of these three agents, urine was the most heavily used." The cleaning consisted of stomping the immersed cloth, rinsing, drying, and pressing it. I'll spare you the details

You can buy issues of Lapham's at Barnes and Noble Bookstore, or you can read it at the public library and borrow recent issues, like "Time," "Travel," and "Swindle and Fraud." They make great icy day reading and help us to forget for a while that, as Nathaniel Ward wrote around 1601, "The world is full of care, much like unto a bubble."

Holes, Moons, and Tea Parties

....

"A Hole Is To Dig: A First Book of Definitions" was the first book I recall reading. It spoke to me so comfortingly, both in its words and pictures, a warm sensation remains all these decades later. The Dictionary of Literary Biography says "A Hole" is "based on the humorous, unexpected definitions children often give things and actions they do not understand." The book begins, "Mashed potatoes are to give everyone enough," with a passel of very small children happily cavorting around an enormous platter of mashed spuds. It was written by Ruth Krauss, one of the giants of American children's literature and can be viewed at **http:// phiwumbda.org/~jesse/geek/functions.html.**

Krauss was part of the legendary Bank Street School staff. The Bank Street concept originated in 1916 with the Bureau of Education Experiments, which was created by visionary educator Lucy Sprague Mitchell. According to the Bank Street website, Mitchell, along with her husband and other like-minded colleagues, began studying young children "to find out what kind of environment is best suited to their learning and growth." They particularly focused on the language and concepts used by children, and after several decades of research, Bank Street staffers began producing picture books that spoke to children like none had before.

A leading example of utilizing children's language in her writing was Mitchell's protégé, Margaret Wise Brown, author of the immortal "Goodnight Moon" and many others before her untimely death doing high kicks too soon after minor surgery. Brown was glamorous, dating celebrities ranging from the Prince of Spain to John Barrymore's wife, and she "lived extravagantly off her royalties."

It was Krauss' editor, Ursula Nordstrom, another, even grander giant of kiddie lit, who showed the "A Hole Is To Dig" manuscript to a window display artist she knew named Maurice Sendak and suggested he submit some illustrations for it. Sendak liked Krauss' words, she liked his sketches, and in 1952 a new classic was born, and he went on to create award-winning classics like "Where the Wild Things Are" and "In the Night Kitchen."

Its unusual, child-like language, doubtlessly inhibited translating "A Hole" effectively into other languages. Since it's such a personal sentimental favorite, I'm glad it's been left alone, especially after reading a recent Wall Street Journal article by Edward Rothstein about the rough treatment Lewis Carroll's "Alice's Adventures in Wonderland" received from international translators.

In the famous Mad Hatter's Tea Party scene, Carroll wrote, "Twinkle, twinkle, little bat!/ How I wonder what you're at!" The French translation reads, "Twinkle, twinkle, little bat!/ What are you doing in the grey evening?" The Croatian version asks, "Flutter, flicker, you little bat!/ Hey, where are you going to go, we'd like to know." It's "Now you twinkle winged rat/ On what are you so concentrated?" in Spanish, in Belarusian it translates as, "Pussycat, pussycat, scream/ With a dumb cry in the night," in Czech it becomes, "A finch was sitting on a stump, a-tooting quietly," and it's, "Along the lake/ Near Mt. Triglav/ A pot drifts," in Slovenian.

Meanwhile scientists have been deconstructing Laura Wilder's "The Little House on the Prairie," according to a recent **Smithsonian.com** article by Michelle Donahue. Titled "The Science of Little House on the Prairie," it describes how "Wilder's reflections on her life experiences have spurred some scientists to use remarkable research techniques to clarify details from the books

that seem a little too incredible." National Weather Service mete-
orologist Barb Boustead, for example, "revisited a Wilder book
from her youth, 'The Long Winter'...she found herself wondering whether the back-to-back blizzards, Wilder wrote about were
as bad as she described...she developed a tool to assign a relative
'badass' score," AKA the Accumulated Winter Season Severity
Index. Boustead found that the winter Laura recalled was indeed
one of the ten worst on record for South Dakota.

Interior Alaskans know all about severe winters, but every season's suited for the Accumulated Reading Memory With a Kid
Index that I just created. Future recollections generated by reading
fun books with a loved ones are truly priceless, and since November
is National Children's Book Month, there's no better time to start
seeking wonderful new children's books in your well-stocked public
library, where you'll also find some long-lost picture book friends,
for as Ruth Krauss wrote, "A book is to look at."

Dashes, Dots, and Librarians

....

The early years of the writing arts contain many aspects that include librarians. Take Butehamen, the next-to-last chief scribe in ancient Egypt's Valley of the Kings. Scribes were the professional predecessors of modern librarians, and it was Butehamen who invented the "bullet," a dot "printed just before a line of type, such as an item in a list, in order to emphasize it." "On the Dot: The Speck That Changed the World," by Alexander and Nicholas Humez, describes how three thousand years ago Butehamen "left faint little red dots…next to each of the short prayers from the Book of the Dead written on the inside of the gesso mummy-cover that was to go inside his own innermost coffin."

My columns must come in under a 700-word limit, so I frequently employ the ellipsis—indicated by three periods (i.e. "…")— to shorten long quotes, like in the preceding sentence. Humez' says that " 'ellipsis' is the practice of leaving a word or words out of a sentence when they are not necessary for understanding it." By the way, the period was also invented by a librarian, Aristophanes of Byzantium, the head librarian at the Alexandrian Library in 200 BCE, who was the first to "put dots in the text to indicate short, medium, and long pauses."

Refurbishing the 1885 Chandler & Price printing press in my garage is one of my retirement projects and pleasures. The pleasurable aspects were heightened recently by attending the Northwoods Book Arts Guild's excellent introductory letterpress class. The big take-away was that setting type—picking out tiny pieces of molded lead and lining them up backwards so they'll print forwards, and distinguishing between tiny inverted "p's" and "q's," "i's" and "l's"– isn't for the impatient or weak-willed. Fortunately, a lifetime in libraries provided some preparation. For example, I know my rectos from my versos and the difference between "em dashes," "en dashes," and hyphens. Your hyphen, the shortest of the three, "connects two things that are intimately related, usually words that function together as a single concept or work together as a joint modifier," like "tie-in" or "toll-free," according to the **ChicagoManualOfStyle.org** Q&A section.

The en dash is longer, about the space that the letter "N" would occupy, and "connects things that are related to each other by distance...which is why they properly appear in indexes when a range of pages is cited (e.g., 147-48)." En dashes also "connect a prefix to a proper open compound: for example, pre-World War II." Meanwhile, the flexible em dash, the size of an "M," can allow "an additional thought to be added within a sentence by sort of breaking away from that sentence—as I've done here." They can also substitute for something missing, like an ellipsis, or bullet point for lists.

"Lorem ipsum," another printer's tool, has arisen several times recently in my Osher Lifelong Learning Institute classes. "Lorem ipsum" are the opening words in a Latin text drawn from Cicero, though intentionally mangled, to act as "filler text commonly used to demonstrate the graphic elements of a document of visual presentation," Wikipedia tells us. "Replacing meaningful content with placeholder text allows viewers to focus on graphic aspects such as font, typography, and page layout without being distracted by the content."

Lorem ipsum is often used for the same purpose by webpage designers. The two words come from the Latin "dolorem ipsum," or "pain itself." Cicero's original passage began, "Neque porro quisquam est qui dolorem ipsum quia dolor sit amet consectetur adipisci velit," which translates as, "Neither is there anyone who loves, pursues or desires pain itself because it is pain." The corrupted form used by printers and web designers reads, "lorem ipsum dolor sit amet consectetur adipisci velit." It was translated for the London Review of Books as "Rrow itself, let it be sorrow; let him pursue it, ishing for its acquisitiendum."

Old Butehamen knew sorrow, for he wrote a poignant letter on a limestone shard and inserted it into the coffin of his dead wife, Ikhtay: "O noble chest of the Osiris... Listen to me and say to her—since you are close to her—"How are you doing? How are you?"

Nonplussed Emojis Not My Fault

....

"**M**ea culpa," or "my fault," is probably my favorite Latin phrase; at least I use it the most. This came to mind while reading a quote from Maxim Gorky, "The most beautiful words in the English language are 'not guilty'." Mea culpas come in two flavors: nouns, used as acknowledgments of guilt, and interjections, or exclamations, as in, "You say that I swore that it's never windy in Interior Alaska in the winter? Mea culpa!" It can be uttered sincerely or snarkily, but not simply as an excuse.

Librarians are exposed to more information than they can retain, but they generally know where to look. Some of us are less retentive than others, and mea culpa came in handy recently when I was asked how many words are in a novel and had no answer off the cuff. Now I do. According to **WritersDigest.com**, "speaking broadly, you can have as few as 71,000 words and as many as 109,000 words… When it dips below 80K, it might be perceived as too short—not giving the reader enough…going over 100K is all right, but not by much…passing 100K in words count means a more expensive book to produce—hence agents' and editors' aversion to such lengths." A 2012 Huffington Post article by Gabe Habash said, "According to Amazon's great Text Stats feature, the median length for all books is about 64,000 words… 'Brave New World's 64,531 word count landed in the exact center of all books."

Sometimes there seem to be too many words running around, and when their meanings shift, as in "nonpluss," it leaves me nonplussed. "Nonplussed" comes from the Latin phrase "non plus," meaning "not more, no further." **OxfordDictionaries.com** says, "In standard use, nonplussed means 'surprised and confused'... In North American English, a new use has developed in recent years, meaning 'unperturbed'—more or less the opposite of its traditional meaning."

Another tradition in December is the naming of the "Word of the Year" by various lexicographical outfits. For example, **OxfordDictionaries.com** named ☺ as its 2015 word-of-the-year. Officially called the "Face with Tears of Joy," ☺ is an emoji, a Japanese word made from "e" (picture), and "moji," (letter). Oxford University Press's analysis of frequency and usage statistics found that ☺ was "the most used emoji globally in 2015. In 2014 it represented 4% of all emojis used in the UK and 9% in the US, but a year later it rose to 20% and 17% respectively. Moreover, usage of the word "emoji" itself also tripled this year.

"So what?" Well, "so" is a term many people are tired of. In exploring how "so" is used, a recent DailyWritingtTips article explained that it's a "discourse marker" an expression "coined in the 1960s to describe 'a word or phrase whose function is to organize discourse into segments and situate a clause, sentence, etc., within a larger context." Examples include, "well," "I see," "you know," "actually," and even "mea culpa." They can initiate discourse ("So, what's up?"), mark a shift in topic or activity ("So, now what?"), begin an explanation ("So, I was walking down the street."), and thereby help buy time to think of what to say.

Using "so" in conversation's one thing, but in formal communications it's problematic. Hunter Thurman, a business consultant," says "so" should be avoided because it insults your audience, undermines your credibility, and makes you seem uncomfortable.

Solid discourse markers were necessary for featured entertainment at rowdy barbarian feasts, and shouting "Hwaet!" got the attention of drunken warriors in the Dark Ages. "Beowulf," the oldest English language poem, begins "Hwaet! We Gar-Dena in gear-dagum, beod-cyninga, brym gerfrunon, hu da aebelingas ellen fremedon!" Or "Listen! We have heard of the might of the kings!" Recently scholars pointed out that there were no exclamation points when Beowulf was written 1,000-1,300 years ago. So in Seamus Heaney's 1999 translation, he begins with "So. The spear-Danes in days gone by and the kings who ruled them had courage and greatness."

There's no need for hwaeting at the library, where, in the words of the Roman playwright Plautus, it's better to "celebrate the occasion with wine and sweet words."

Old Books, Old Librarians, and Literary Iceland

....

There's much to commend about old books, beginning with the observation of Victorian critic John Ruskin, "All books are divisible into two classes: the books of the hour, and the books of all time." Some old books possess monetary value, but most, apart from sentimental regard, are worth maybe a dollar. Back in my librarying days, people occasionally asked me to appraise their dusty tomes.

I couldn't, not possessing a certified appraiser's skill and experience, but I knew a few things. For example, a jillion editions of the works of Twain, Dickens, etc. were published in the late 1800s when the blooming of the industrial revolution fueled the rapid growth of reading. Today such books are generally worth a few bucks at most. Those curious about a book's value can start by checking out their book's price range at **BookFinder.com**, which gathers listings from hundreds of private book dealers, as well as Powell's, Amazon, ABE, and other online used book venders.

But you never know. Once a Texas school teacher asked me to look at a half-dozen books she'd inherited. They looked like nothing special, but later a rare book dealer in Austin found that the papers lining the inside of one of the book's bindings was made from Revolutionary War currency. A few months ago a map of Tolkien's Middle Earth that had been hand-annotated by Tolkien himself was found stuffed inside a copy of "Lord of the Rings" owned by the English illustrator Pauline Baynes. She had illustrated the Middle Earth map found in most editions of Tolkien's books, and they discussed it during a visit he made to her in 1969. Apparently while they chatted, he doodled on a print of Baynes' map and indicated that Hobbiton and Oxford were at the same latitude, the Italian city of Ravenna inspired the fictional city of Minas Tirith, and Belgrade and Jerusalem all figured into the Middle Earth landscape. The auction house expects the map to bring 60,000 pounds.

An assistant professor of English also made an impressive find last October, according to a NY Times article titled, "Earliest Known Draft of King James Bible Is Found." Jeffrey Miller was poking around the Cambridge University archives last year when he came across "an unassuming notebook about the size of a modern paperback, wrapped in a stained piece of waste velum and filled with some 70 pages of Ward's nearly indecipherable handwriting" dating from 1604-8. Samuel Ward was one of the King James Bible (KJB) translators, and he possessed such awful handwriting librarians had misconstrued the little book as a biblical commentary. Actually, Miller had found the KJB's "earliest known draft, and the only one definitively written in the hand of one of the roughly four-dozen translators who worked on it."

David Norton, a leading KJB expert "called it 'a major discovery'—if not quite equal to finding a draft of one of Shakespeare's plays, 'getting on up there."

Studies repeatedly show that humans appreciate many aspects of books, especially their odor. Guess what? A **CNN.com** article from last April said, "New research indicates that 'Double Falsehood,' a play first published in 1728 by Lewis Theobald, was actually written more than a century earlier by Shakespeare himself, with help from his friend John Fletcher. University of Texas researchers "analyzed 33 plays by Shakespeare, nine by Fletcher, and 12 by Theobald to create a 'psychological signature' of each author based on word choices, phrase patterns, and other factors…the play's first half was almost entirely written by Shakespeare, though the second half appeared to be split evenly between Shakespeare and Fletcher. Only tiny traces of Theobald's signature were found." "Double

Falsehood" is also known as "The Distressed Lovers" and is based on the "Cardeno" section of Cervantes' "Don Quixote."

The best way to pass along potentially valuable books for future generations is give them today. They do this better in Iceland than anywhere. An online article by Giulia Trentacosti described Iceland's Jolabokaflod, or "Christmas book flood," festival. The majority of Iceland's books are published around Christmastime, and it's become a tradition to exchange new and used books then. The flood of books comes from the fact that Iceland is so literate. "With around 330,000 inhabitants, Iceland is certainly one of the smallest book markets in the world. Nevertheless, it boasts one of the highest rates of books per capita (3.5 books every 1,000 inhabitants)." They also each read an average of eight books annually, and "an impressive 98% read at least one."

Exchanging holiday books is an old Hill family tradition, and that includes old collectable comic books. Sometimes, as American sage Ralph Emerson noted, "Old age is a good advertisement."

Petting, Sweating, and Spizzarinctum

....

George Carlin once advised, "Don't sweat the petty things, and don't pet the sweaty things," which led me pondering the word "sweater." It was coined in 1828 to mean "clothing worn to produce sweat and reduce weight," and a few years later "sweater" meant "rower's garb," all stemming from its meaning in the 1520s of "one who works hard." We can thank Lana Turner, whose appearance in the 1937 movie, "They Won't Forget," for being the first "sweater girl."

"Spizzarinctum," a term meaning "zest for life," or "to instill a win to succeed," was a special favorite of my Dad's. In the mid-1800 America "spizzarinctum" (sic) meant "money in coin form," but, according to a 2005 Jewish World Review article, "spizzerinktum" (sic) was defined in a 1944 book of U.S. Marine slang as "intestinal fortitude." That's certainly how my Dad, a Marine on Guadalcanal in WWII, defined it often enough to instill that and many other expressions peculiar to Marines into our family lexicon.

It was B.J. Palmer, the founder of chiropractic medicine, who first popularized spizzarinctum in the 1920s. The Google Book Ngram Viewer is a free online search engine that charts how frequently words and phrases are found in books, newspapers, and other printed sources between 1500 and 2008, and it produces graphs showing particular words' popularity. "Spizzarinctum," for instance is shown emerging in the 1920s and skyrocketing in popularity in the 40s and 50s as the Marines and other servicemen returned to civilian life.

It's rumored that spizzarinctum was derived from a Latin phrase, "specie rectum," literally translated as "the right kind." However, the Jewish World Review article debunked the theory saying "that etymology appears to be a misguided attempt to make something more of good old American slang than is warranted." What should be warranted in our political discussions is using "and" more and "but" less. In "Woodrow Wilson Was a Racist, But He Deserves Our Understanding," Washington Post columnist Richard Cohen described current efforts to expunge Wilson's name from the Princeton University campus he ran from 1902-1910 due to his avowed racist tendencies without consideration of some noble aspects of his character. "What's lacking," Cohen wrote, "is an appreciation of the word 'and.' Instead, 'but' is too often substituted, so that a person becomes one or the other—not two things at once."

"Debt" got similar treatment. It comes to English from the French "dette," which originated in the Latin "debitum," or "thing owed." Over the past few centuries English grammarians shoe-horned a "B" back into the term as part of their efforts to make English words and usage conform to Latin's logical orderliness, even though that made our already confusing language even more Byzantine. The "R" sound in "colonel" is another example of this. As **A.Word.A.Day** author Anu Garg noted, "we borrowed (from French and Italian) two variants of the term: colonel and coronel. After a period of trying out both, we decided to keep the spelling from one and pronunciation from the other. While talking about colonels, a colonel is, literally, a little column, because he heads a column of soldiers."

It's a relief knowing that sharing these verbal insights helps me be mentally healthy. "Smartasses Are More Creative and Have Greater Psychological Well-being," an online article by Corey Clark, reported that a study from Harvard and Columbia Business Schools found that, "Instead of being the lowest form of wit, it seems that sarcastic humor is actually employed by those whose intellects soar in more lofty realms. On top of this, it was found that the liberal use of sarcastic comments can help lift the I.Q.s of the less intellectually well-endowed." "Sarcasm," Clark continued, "is based on irony, word play, and multiple meanings. It takes brain power to come up with sarcastic comments. The listener is forced to decipher what was meant instead of what was actually said." Library frequenters must have such smartass tendencies and attributes, too, because they're regularly exercising their brains, and their intellects often consequently "soar into more lofty realms." Many of them will appreciate knowing that the Ngram Viewer can compare multiple terms simultaneously. For example, a comparison of "awesome," "splendid," "terrific," and "amazing" revealed the expression being overused at present, "awesome," came in as a slender fraction when compared historically to "splendid" and "amazing." "Terrific," a word I recall hearing often in my youth but seldom these days, is down there with "awesome" and "superb."

Each of those adjectives can be applied to our marvel-filled library, where smart people find spizzarinctum every day.

Yogi, Gene, and Norman

....

Once Yogi Berra was explaining a particularly awful Yankees outing: "We made too many wrong mistakes." A similar case in point was reported recently in a **WashingtonPost.com** article titled, "Londoners Accidentally Pay For Free Wi-Fi with a Firstborn, Because No One Reads Anymore." That's right, "[i]n an experiment sponsored by security firm F-Secure, an open Wi-Fi network was set up in a busy public area. When people connected, they were presented with lengthy terms and conditions. But to see just how little attention we pay when checking that agreement box, F-Secure included a 'Herod clause,'" that meant checking the "I agree" box gave the company full rights to the WiFi subscribers' firstborn children.

A few years earlier another British company pulled the same trick in which those agreeing signed away "their immortal souls." The problem is that "Internet users actually read only about 20 percent of the words they 'read.' We've convinced ourselves that we're master speed readers, but we're actually just skimming."

A **ScienceDaily.com** article from a week ago cites research from the Journal of the American Medical Association that "[e]lectronic toys for infants that produce lights, words, and songs were associated with decreased quantity and quality of language compared to playing with books or traditional toys... Children also vocalized less while playing with electronic toys than with books... These results add to the large body of evidence supporting the potential benefits of book reading with very young children."

Another common digital mistake was reported in another **WashingtonPost.com** article titled "study Confirms That Ending Your Texts With a Period Is Terrible." Ending text messages with periods is "perceived as being less sincere, probably because the people sending them are heartless." However, "exclamation points—once a rather uncouth punctuation mark—may make your messages seem more sincere than no punctuation at all."

An overwhelming number of studies have shown that using digital devices to teach reading is a huge mistake, but so is putting all your literary eggs into one basket. Not long ago many people thought that the e-book innovation meant the end of print books, yet today more print books are being published than ever before, while e-books sales have stagnated for several years. Nonetheless, digital books are far easier to store, transport, and sift through for specific words. I own an e-reader that's great for traveling with a small library of beloved books, but I also own their print versions, too, because I want to remember them, and digital reading inhibits that.

"Books In 2015: From Coloring Books to Harper Lee, A Good Year For Paper," a recent News Miner article, noted that "Paper all along has been especially popular for nonfiction and children's books." That's why the Alaska Guys and Gals Read programs introduces 4th graders—the age when most boys stop reading for pleasure—to heavily-illustrated print books that are brimming with fun. Local adult volunteers read these books during school lunchtimes while projecting the pages so everyone can follow along. Then copies of the books are donated to the school libraries. The program's innovative approach was created here in Fairbanks and has proven amazingly successful at engaging the kids in reading for fun, winning multiple national awards.

It's fitting that cartoonist Gene Yang, the renowned author of the graphic novel "American Born Chinese," has been appointed Ambassador for Young People's Literature by the Library of

Congress. Mr. Yang is the son of Chinese immigrants, and grew up in San Francisco Bay. He began drawing at 2. One of Yang's boyhood pals is Jason Shiga, author of "Meanwhile," definitely the best choose-your-own-adventure book ever. "Meanwhile" was featured by Guys Read several years ago, and Mr. Shiga came to Fairbanks, at no charge, to appear at local schools and the Guys Read parties held at the public library.

That's because he agrees that developing a love of reading in children is too important to mess up. Guys and Gals Read have proven exceptionally effective at doing that. And as Norman Vincent Peale noted, "We've all heard that we have to learn from our mistakes, but I think it's more important to learn from your successes."

Messiness, Disgust, and Reproduction

....

Why do I find titles like "Rats, Exploding Sewers, and Demons of the Deep: The Hazards of Roman Sewers" completely irresistible, while my spouse can resist them absolutely? "Disgust Dampens Women's Sexual Arousal More Than Fear," a recent **ScienceDaily.com** article, proved equally alluring, and perhaps a bit revelatory. "Being disgusted is a bigger passion killer for women than fear, according to new research," it stated. Surprisingly, the study "is the first to use medical equipment in addition to self-reporting."

"It makes sense that sexual arousal and disgust would affect one another," according to the article. "Sexual arousal motivates us toward closeness with others and their bodies while disgust moves us away. Given these competing motivations, every one of our ancestors had to overcome disgust in order…to reproduce."

Unsurprisingly, the report also found that one "of the most consistent differences science has found between men and women is that men are less sensitive to disgust than women, especially when it comes to sex." Perhaps it all figures into Arizona State researcher Melissa Wilson Sayres' study, described in an **IFLSScience.com** article, that she discovered that, right when agriculture was discovered and villages began to be invented—about 4,000-8,000 years ago—an average of 17 women passed along their genes compared to each man. This happened all over the world, yet there's no evidence of a virus or other natural calamity causing it.

The culprit's probably creeping civilization., Sayers said, "[i]nstead of 'survival of the fittest' in a biological sense, the accumulation of wealth and power may have increased the reproductive success of a limited number of 'socially fit' males and their sons." Other research has found that "[a]lmost all parents say they don't favor one of their children over another, but economic recessions subconsciously lead parents to prefer girls over boys."

A **ScienceDaily.com** article quoted Vladas Griskevicius of Rutger Business School saying "[t]hese findings in humans align well with the behavior of other animals. When resources are scarce parents prefer females because they have larger reproductive payoff. Almost every female child will produce some offspring, but many male children end up having zero offspring." For example, the study looked at the nation's retail spending on apparel for boys 1984 and 2011 and discovered that "when the economy was struggling, the ration of spending on girls versus boys increased 19.8 percent compared to when the economy was faring well."

It's worth noting that in economic hard times, like in Alaska right now, males and females both need public libraries more than ever, turning to them for job information, entertainment, education, and more. Even in good economies, a majority of Americans of all walks of life rely on their libraries to help bolster their families, livelihoods, and lifestyles.

Meanwhile, researchers are expanding their study of that genetic dip 4,000-8,000 years ago to find why those prehistoric farmers stopped reproducing. Maybe they were simply too disgusting. My personal workspaces have been termed messy, and worse, to some. How delightful to read the recent **Independent.com** article, "Why being messy can be a positive trait," that cites a recent University of Wisconsin study that found while "working at a neat, tidy desk may make a person more likely to eat healthily and be more generous, a messier desk can promote creativity and help give birth to ideas."

The study was published in the journal "Psychological Science," and its authors said, [m]essy desks may not be as detrimental as they appear to be, as the problem-solving approaches they seem to cause can boost work efficiency or enhance employees' creativity in problem solving." How can this be? The authors of the book "A Perfect Mess: The Hidden Benefits of Disorder"—which is available at your public library—noted that "the 'more important, urgent work lurks at the top of the clutter,' while the 'safely ignorable stuff' falls to the bottom." Makes sense to me.

Otherwise, I blame defective URB-597. An irresistible article titled, "Scientist discover a difference between the sexes," said a Northwestern University study has learned that "[m]ale and female brains operate a different molecular level." A substance known as URB-597 apparently affects women's brains more than men's by heightening the synapse responses in the brain's hippocampus region that regulates "a variety of physiological processes including memory, motivational state, appetite, and pain.".

That could explain my crappy memory, messiness, and, perhaps, my insatiable appetite for reading.

Smelly Books, Double Falsehoods, and Categorical Thinking

....

Science fiction legend Ray Bradbury once wrote, "A book has got smell. A new book smells great. An old book smells even better. An old book smells like ancient Egypt." Of course, some books are smellier than others. Scientists say those odors are caused by volatile organic compounds, or VOCs, that comprise the book's paper, ink and glue. According to **IFLScience.com**, "over time, the VOCs break down, releasing the chemicals into the air." Book VOC aromas include "hints of almond," "notes of vanilla," and "a light floral fragrance."

As librarians know all too well, "the book can also retain some odors it has been exposed to during its history, such as smoke, water damage, or pressed flowers between the pages." I've seen raw bacon and lunchmeat used as bookmarks in returned library books, along with exceedingly personal letters and photos, and even money, such as the time some anonymous person returned a book containing the exact cash from that year's permanent fund check.

Sometimes the odors aren't so sweet, so here's advice from **ILAB. org**, the International League of Antiquarian Booksellers on how to get rid of book reek. Find a clean container just bigger than the smelly book, and another, larger container that's also clean. Inside the larger one put plenty of baking soda, kitty litter, charcoal brickettes, or other odor-absorbing agents. Stand the book upright in the smaller container with the pages fanned out. Then place it all in the larger one and close the lid. Leave it there for several days or until the smell's gone.

Stinkiness comes in all shapes and sizes. Consider Lewis Theobald, a British author and editor who lived in the early 1700s and did some important work editing Shakespeare's plays. One sad day Theobald criticized the new edition of Shakespeare's works edited by the poet Alexander Pope. Pope was irked and wrote "The Dunciad," a satire on the contemporary British literary scene. The King of the Dunces was named Tibbald, one pronunciation of Theobald's name. Pope included the nastiest gossip on Theobald, provided evidence of his plagiarism and claimed that he wrote anonymous letters to publications in praise of himself. The Wikipedia article on him notes that "Pope succeeded in so utterly obliterating the character of the man that he is known by those who do not work with Shakespeare only as a dunce, as a dusty, pedantic, and dull witted scribe."

Theobald published a play appropriately called "Double Falsehood" in 1728 claiming "to have based the play on three original Shakespeare manuscripts... The manuscripts have since been lost, presumably in a library fire," according to a **ScienceDaily. com** article. The debate's raged over who actually wrote what ever since Pope's and Theobald's era. Then last April "the Shakespeare algorithm" was invented at the University of Texas by researchers James Pennebaker and Ryan Boyd. They "examined 33 plays by Shakespeare, 12 by Theobald, and 9 by John Fletcher, a colleague of Shakespeare, and sometimes his collaborator. The texts were stripped of extraneous information (such as publication information) and were processed using software that evaluated the works for specific features."

Pennebaker and Boyd wrote that "the psychological style and content architecture predominantly resemble those of Shakespeare, showing some similarity with Fletcher's signature, and only traces of Theobald's. For example, the researchers' software examined the playwrights' use of function words (e.g. pronouns, articles, prepositions) and words belonging to various content categories (e.g. emotions, family, sensory perception, religion). They had the software identify themes present in each of the works to generate an overarching thematic signature for each author." They also examined the plays for "categorical writing." Categorical thinkers "tend to be emotionally distant, applying problem-solving approaches to everyday situations. People who rate low on categorical thinking, on the other hand, tend to live in the moment and are more focused on social matters."

I won't guess where I am on that spectrum, but will take my stinky, old beat-up Riverside Edition of Shakespeare's works with me to read at Fairbanks Shakespeare Theatre's 17th annual Bard-a-thon that's going on round the clock all this week at Raven Landing. I'm aiming to read "All's Well," where the clown says, "Indeed sir, if your metaphor stink, I will stop my nose; or against any man's metaphor."

OMG, Dord, and Circumflex Perplexion

....

Sometimes lawlessness works. Compare the practically unfettered, free-for-all English language with the highly-regulated French language. New words enter English all the time, but the Academie Francaise, "the watchdog of the French Language,"—whose members are known as "The Immortals"—oversees all official alterations to their language. The most recent Academie-inspired uproar came when they decided to make "[c]hanges to around 2,400 French words to simplify them for school children, such as allowing the word for onion to be spelled 'ognon' as well as the traditional oignon," according to a recent **TheGuardian.com** article by Kim Wilsher. "The aim was to standardize and simplify certain quirks in the written language, making it easier to learn."

The most controversial change was the removal of the little tent-shaped circumflex sign (^) over the letters I and U "where the accent does not change the pronunciation or meaning of the word." "In French," Wikipedia says, "the circumflex generally marks the former presence of a consonant, usually 's', that was deleted and no longer pronounced. A no-brainer, right? Within hours a Twitter account called #JeSuisCirconflexe, "derived from the #JeSuisCharlie hashtag" that went viral following the terrorist shootings at the French magazine several years ago. Then the far right Front National political party attacked the Immortals' spelling changes, declaring "the French language is our soul."

The Academie actually approved these changes unanimously

back in 1990, but no one noticed until this month when a television reported about the school textbook publishers' decision to
incorporate the spelling changes. Within days the "growing fury
forced the education ministry in France to reassure the public…that
the circumflex accent was not disappearing, and that even though
school textbooks would be standardized to contain new spellings,
pupils using either would be given full marks."

Of course, the relative porosity of our tongue means words enter
the English lexicon in the strangest ways. A former colleague at our
local library recently sent me a document containing the news that
February 28 will be 85th anniversary of the demise of the term
"dord." On this date a Webster's New International Dictionary
editor noticed that the entry for "dord" was missing an etymology
describing its origins. It turned out that "'dord' had no etymology
because it wasn't a word. In 1931 a slip reading 'D or d, cont. density,' which meant to add 'density' to the list of terms abbreviated
as 'D,' was misread as 'Dord' during the compilation of the dictionary's next edition. and was filed as a separate word. Eventually,
through sheer inertia, 'dord' acquired a part of speech, 'n.,' and a
pronunciation."

Confession time. Patrick O'Brian, my favorite author, is known
for the precise historical accuracy of the events he describes, as
well as the richness and hidden treasures he salted throughout the
20-volume Aubrey-Maturin series, his 7,000-page masterpiece. I'm
forever re-reading these great novels, and in the current one I'm
enjoying, "Fortunes of War," a protagonist named Maturin asked an
American medical colleague the meaning of the American expression he'd overheard: "That cuts no ice with me." "After barely
a moment's pause, Mr. Evans said, "Ah, there now, you have an
Indian expression. It is a variant upon the Iroquois 'katno aiss'
vizmi'—I am unmoved, unimpressed."

Naturally, I took Mr. O'Brian at his word, for he was an
imminent researcher honored by the British National Library by
being the only author to have a novel published by them. Then

WorldWideWords.org told me "You have fallen victim to Mr. O'Brian's droll sense of humor... The supposed Iroquois expression is, of course, just a respelled version of the English." They go on to say that "cuts no ice" wasn't recorded until the late 1800s, but I began spreading O'Brian's version as gospel in the late 1990s.

There's lexicographical backup you can rely upon when I tell you that the ubiquitous Internet expressions "OMG" and "LOL" weren't the brainchildren of teenaged girls. In 1960 "LOL" meant "little old lady," and the library's beloved Oxford English Dictionary insists on listing "Lots Of Love" as one meaning, because it's what some of us fogeys still think when encountering LOLs online. The first recorded use of "OMG" came in an excited letter from an Admiral Jacky Fisher to Winston Churchill in 1917, stating "I hear that a new order of Knighthood is on the tapis—O.M.G (Oh! My! God!)." Or as French traditionalists prefer saying, "sacrebleu."

Rudeness, Cakewalks, and Library Fines

....

This era of political and cultural rudeness is certainly nothing new. In the latter 1600s French philosopher Jean de la Bruyere castigated his contemporaries' widespread rudeness, saying, "Incivility is not a Vice of the soul, but the effect of several Vices; of Vanity, Ignorance, of Duty, Laziness, Stupidity, Distraction, Contempt of others, and Jealousy." Not being above rudeness himself, his main work was "The Characters: of the Manners of the Age," wherein he defined "qualities such as dissimulation, flattery, or rusticity" and gave examples drawn from unnamed but real people ostensibly "for the purpose of reforming manners." Figuring out who la Bruyere was describing became a popular Parisian pastime, and made him many enemies.

Another form of instructive rudeness comes from grammar Nazis. "Are You a Grammar Pedant? This Might Be Why," an article by David Shariatmadari in last week's **TheGuardian.com** described research into why some people are hypersensitive to "typos" ("mistakes that can be attributed to the slip of the finger") and "grammos" ("errors involving knowledge of the rules of language"). They found that extroverts tend to be the most forgiving of others' grammar errors, while introverts "are more likely to get annoyed at both typos and grammos," and are more likely to abruptly correct grammar transgressors.

Some rudeness is discreet. An example arose during a class I took through Osher Lifelong Learning class on English country dancing—that Jane Austen style of dancing in long lines facing your partner and taking turns parading down the middle of the rows—when I recalled silent films showing the African-American dance craze of the 1800s: cakewalking.

Seeking possible connections, I did some librarying and found an academic paper by Meghan Hilbruner titled "It Ain't No Cake Walk: the Influence of African American Music and Dance on the American Cultural Landscape." "The original Cakewalk, as we know from oral tradition, was a dance that imitated the style of dance slaves saw their masters perform," Hilbruner wrote. "The dance slaves imitated was from the early 1800s, known as the Georgian or Regency period... The enslaved folk saw these dances when serving at parties held in the big house. Enslaved folk found the intricate and stiff dancing funny and 'high mannered'... Cakewalk dances involved high steps and jumps...it exaggerated the small skips and hops in the white dancing." The white masters failed "to realize that the enslaved folk were not learning out of interest in the whites' dance, but in mockery of it."

Once tea parties were considered rude. According to "When Sipping Tea Was a Socially Ruinous Act," an **AtlasObscura.com** article by Hillary Meares, "there was a time when tea was seen as a threat to Christian values and the social hierarchy of the Western World." When introduced to Europe in the 1500s, tea was prohibitively expensive early on, but prices dropped and soon British commoners began consuming the brew. Tea parties provided women chances to congregate and socialize, thus leading their male contemporaries to fear a rise in "general domestic irresponsibility," and a "threat to national instability."

Actually the guys weren't far wrong. A group of women including Elizabeth Cady Stanton had a tea party in July 1848. "I poured out, that day, the torrent of my long-accumulated discontent," Stanton remembered, "with such vehemence and indignation that I stirred myself, as well as the rest of the party, to do and dare anything." A few weeks later the women's rights movement, which many people considered quite rude, was launched at a convention of women, including Stanton, at Seneca Falls.

Shameful rudeness is achieved when libraries become too expensive to use. Last week the NY Times reported on how $.50/day late fees charged by the public library of San Jose, CA are prohibiting 39% of all users from borrowing books or using the library computers. Half of the city's children, mostly from low-income families, have unaffordable overdue fines. A cost-benefit analysis prepared by our library at former Assemblyperson Bonnie Williams request that showed that the our library's policy to not charge overdue fines actually saved money after figuring in the costs associated with handling petty cash and replacing books that were never returned by delinquent borrowers.

It may sound like a small thing, but not having fines creates good feelings. As Ann Taylor wrote, "One ugly trick has often spoiled/ The sweetest and the best."

Grammar, Style, and Nonpologies

....

"**M**any English speakers cannot understand basic grammar" was the headline of a **ScienceDailyNews.com** article several years ago citing research out of Britain's Northumbria University that found that people who dropped out of school by age 16 had far more difficulty understanding simple sentences that were written in the passive voice instead of the active voice. Sentences expressed passively treat nouns that would be the object of an active sentence as the subject. For example, "Caesar was stabbed by Brutus" is passive, but "Brutus stabbed Caesar" is active.

The Northumbria researchers "stressed that the findings had nothing to do with intelligence," and many of the test subjects who were given training after the tests picked up the distinction between passive and active voices quickly. However, I noted this came from NORTHumbria. Most Southerners admit that our indirect way of approaching most topics is usually politely passive. Even after a quarter-century in Alaska, I'm still taken aback when plain-speaking—I might even say, abrupt—Northerners tell me just what they think.

It's so incredibly easy to confound one another linguistically that it's a good thing stylebooks were invented. "Stylebook" is defined by the American Heritage Dictionary as a " book giving rules and examples of usage, punctuation, and typography used in preparing copy for publication." The Associated Press Stylebook on Media Law, or AP Stylebook, for instance, "is a writing style guide for journalists… It provides fundamental guidelines for spelling, language, punctuation, usage, and journalistic style. It is the definitive resource for journalists," according to **APStylebook.com**. The website includes an "Ask the Editor" section where subscribers can pose specific questions. For example, a recent inquirer asked "Does a Senator serve IN the Senate or ON the Senate?" The answer was "A senator serves in the Senate and on a Senate committee," thereby subtly correcting the improper capitalization of "senator."

That person could have contacted their public library and gotten the same answer for free. Not being an AP subscriber, I can't say with certainty, but I presume it contains precious little relating to Alaska. That's why the library and I both own copies of "The Associated Press Stylebook for Alaska" compiled by former UAF professor Dean Gottehrer, and why I can say with certainty that it's journalistically OK to call the Yukon Quest International Sled Dog Race simply "the Quest." Still, it should be mentioned that Gottehrer's stylebook makes a point of the odd spelling of Anchorage's Loussac Library, but fails to note Noel Wien Library's equally unusual spelling

The light-hearted "Stylebook of Leviticus" from **IrishTimes. com** is one of the more amusing stylebooks, with edicts such as, "Use not an apostrophe in the possessive 'its', that is unclean to ye", "Touch not the word 'iconic', for except in a small number of cases. It is unclean as a sheep's buttocks," and "Confuse not the transitive verb 'lay' with the intransitive 'lie'. For if ye do, ye shall surely go the way of the false prophet Bob Dylan, who urgeth his woman to 'Lay Lady Lay,' as if she be a hen or a goose or any other fowl after its kind. That is an abomination and he that committeth it must be punished. For did not the Dylanites themselves say: 'Everybody must get stoned?' And in this case, at least, they spake the truth."

Sometimes, like President U.S. Grant, we must acknowledge that "Mistakes were made." However, this is a prime example of weasel-speak that's been utilized by later politicians, notably, according to quotations source books, Presidents Reagan and Nixon. Known as a "non-apology apology," or "nonpology." According to Wikipedia, a nonpology is "A statement that has the form of an apology but does not express the expected contrition. In "Effective Apology" John Kador wrote, "Adding the word 'if' or any other conditional modifier to an apology makes it a non-apology."

We'll close with a compelling argument from **McSweeney's. net's** "Interactive Guide to Ambiguous Grammar" for you active voice strict-constructionists. "[L]anguage is an art of nuance. From time to time, writers may well find illustrative value in the lightest of phrases, sentences so weightless and feathery that they scarcely even seem to exist at all. These can convey details well beyond the crude thrust of the hulking active voice." Still not convinced? I'm sorry if you feel that way.

Prisons, Libraries and Bug-eating Coaches

Several interesting points emerged during my time in the Arizona Territorial Prison, once known for being both a "hell hole" or a "country club." A recent visit to Yuma, AZ included a tour of the old prison there that operated from 1876 to 1909. The hellish parts stemmed from aspects such as the oppressive heat, rampant tuberculosis, and surrounding quicksand pits. However, a few of its early prison superintendents believed in rehabilitation as much as punishment, and many non-prison residents of Yuma resented the convicts enjoying amenities they didn't have, such as electricity, plumbing, showers, and a library.

The Yuma Prison Library was created in 1883 during the administration of superintendent F.S. Ingalls, who also opened blacksmith, carpentry, cobbler, and tailor shops to teach inmates job skills. The prison library was the brainchild of his wife, Madora Ingalls, who raised funds to buy the library's furniture and 2,000 books. Some consider it the first library in the Arizona Territory. "Dora" Ingalls was well-known among the convicts for raising money for a prison band, tending sick prisoners, and other kindnesses; that's why they were surprised when she once successfully manned a Lowell Battery Gun, similar to the Gatlin Gun, to quell a mass breakout attempt.

The prison closed in 1909 when a new, larger one opened elsewhere, but the facility was utilized as the local high school from 1910-14 when the old school burned. Visiting sports teams taunted the Yuma athletes by calling them "criminals," but the aspersion was embraced by the students, and Yuma High remains home to the Fighting Criminals.

Living in the Yuma prison was tough for guards and inmates, and it's unsurprising that the occupation of corrections officer is one of the lowest-rated in the annual "2015 Jobs Rated Report" from **CareerCast.com**, "the Internet's premier career site for finding targeted job opportunities." The report looks at earnings, stress, and prospective job growth to determine a best-worst compilation of 200 jobs in 2015. With 200 being the worst, corrections officer came in at 194. Enlisted military, lumberjack and newspaper reporter bottomed out at 198-200, respectively, while farmer and garbage collector tied at 180. Funeral director and attorney came in at 124-125, bartender and nurse at 118-119, and hairstylist, parole officer, and nuclear engineer at 79-80-81.

Librarians were up there at 35, but actuary, audiologist, mathematician and statistician topped the heap at 1-4. I was glad to see historian make 43, though this was a huge drop from 2010, when historian were ranked 5. Lord knows more historians are needed since a Washington (St. Louis) University study found that 71% of Americans think Alexander Hamilton was a U.S. president, while "Franklin Pierce and Chester Arthur were recognized less than 60% of the time," according to the report in **ScienceDaily.com**. Apparently we do OK recalling the first few and the recent presidents, but after that, watch out. Over 25% of Americans think Ben Franklin, Hubert Humphrey, and 16th century theologian Thomas More were all presidents.

Some history, like baseball cards, can be pleasantly ephemeral. The baseball card boom busted in 1994, the year of the infamous players' strike, when 81 billion cards were issued—"325 cards for every man woman, and child in the U.S."—and the cost rose from 50 cents to $3-4 per pack. Most sports cards have little or no value, but some certainly do. A recent **NPR.org** article described a family going through some deceased great-grandparents' belongings found seven rare Ty Cobb cards from 1909-11—in a crumpled paper bag—that are estimated to be worth "well into seven figures."

I prize my old baseball card collection and had to get it down after reading Grant Bisbee's amusing article titled "The 11 Genres of Baseball Photos" in **SBNation.com**, a sports news blog. The players featured on the cards are posed in finite ways: batting, swinging, smiling headshot, etc. Bisbee identified several new groupings, like "Floating Ball," where the player has tossed a ball up by his head, and "Coach Eating a Bug," in which painfully uncomfortable coaches produce intriguing pop-eyed expressions.

My collection includes a group I call "What's In His Mouth," and categories like "What's He Looking At, and "Ugly Man." They're worth little except to me, and as English historian Thomas Carlyle noted, "In a certain sense, all men are historians."

Cheecks, Civility, and Logofocos

Cats and dogs are very different creatures, yet, with some exceptions, they can get along together civilly, as evidenced by a long series of both critters cohabitating my household. There are some similarities; both are predators and natural biters, and neither possesses full cheeks. And "without cheeks, they can't create suction to drink, as people, horses, and elephants do," according to "Precise Method Underlies Sloppy Madness of Dog Slurping," a recent **ScienceDaily.com** article. Instead, "they use their tongues to quickly raise water upward through a process involving inertia."

"Both animals move their tongues too quickly to be completely observed by the naked eye. But dogs accelerate their tongues at a much faster rate than cats, plunging them into the water and curling them downward toward their lower jaws, not their noses. They quickly retract their tongues and a column of water forms and rises into their mouths, but they also curl the underside of their tongues to bring a tiny ladle of water upward. Cats, on the other hand, lightly touch the surface of the water with their tongues, never fully immersing them... When their tongues rise into their mouths, liquid adheres to the upper side, forming an elegant water column."

All full-cheeked humans suck and drink the same way. It seems we'd be better at talking civilly, too, like Black Tom Fairfax, one of the most civil leaders during the English Civil War. I encountered Fairfax in John Aubrey's "Brief Lives," in which he gave scores of thumbnail personality sketches of "Worthies of England" as they were seen in the mid-1600s. Aubrey's book works wonders at putting me to sleep, but reading Aubrey's 100-word entry on "Thomas Fairfax, 1612-1671," woke me right up: "Thomas, Lord Fairfax of Cameron [was] Lord General of the Parliament Army" that besieged the King's army in the town of Oxford. "When Oxford was surrendered (24 June 1646), the first thing General Fairfax did was to set a good guard of soldiers to protect the Bodleian Library." After describing the abuses the Bodleian had suffered at the hand of the King's Cavaliers when they controlled Oxford, "by embezzling and cutting off chains of books," Aubrey noted that Fairfax "was a lover of learning, and had he not taken special care, that noble library had been utterly destroyed... I assure you this from an ocular witness."

The Bodleian is one of the world's greatest libraries, founded in 1602 and eventually incorporating the libraries of all the colleges making up Oxford University. Since 1610 a copy of every book published in Britain has to be given to the Bodleian, which now has over 110 miles of shelves. Like most of the world's gigantic libraries, you can read, but not borrow, their millions of books in one of the 29 ornate reading rooms. And you have to ask a librarian to retrieve it for you well in advance of your visit; in other words, no browsing the bookstacks.

Oliver Cromwell was an extremist, and Fairfax's underling, and was less willing to consider both sides of issues and remember the underlying humanity of everyone involved. Fairfax's reputation for moderation was such that he was forgiven when the monarchy was restored, while other Parliament leaders lost their heads. Speaking of which, what's with calling the criminal who harassed the Iditarod mushers with a snowmachine a "terrorist?" Calling a drunken fool "a terrorist," with its implication that he plotted his attack, had premeditated evil intent, or even desired it at all when sober, is extreme hyperbole, a form of verbal terrorism, that sadly reflects the national mood.

It's part of a miserable cycle, like the Locofoco Party of 1830s America. "Loco-Foco" was a "self-lighting cigar" patented in 1834, with "loco" coming from "locomotion" and "foco" being a mis-spelling of "fuoco," Italian for "fire." It quickly came to mean self-igniting matches, like those used by a radical wing of the Democratic Party to light candles when the angry Democratic Party bosses turned off the gaslights in their meeting hall. Ralph Waldo Emerson said the Locofocos were "stiff, heady, and rebel-lious; they are fanatics in freedom; they hate tolls, taxes, turnpikes, banks, hierarchies, governors, yea, almost all laws." Sounds like the modern political scene. Fortunately, we possess public libraries dedicated to presenting all viewpoints to foster an informed, civil electorate, because sometimes even dogs and cats need to get along.

Tigernuts, Shopping Lists, and Animal Skin

....

Tigernut Sweets may be on my menu soon. I read about this extremely old recipe on **AncientNile.co.uk**, where I also learned that no ancient peoples are known to have had cookbooks. Some recipes from those days survived long enough to be written down including the intriguingly-named Tigernuts, which are made by making a paste of dates and water, adding lots of cinnamon and chopped walnuts, and rolling it into balls, dipping them in honey, and finally rolling them in ground almonds.

The Egyptians might have struggled along without cookbooks, but not Fairbanksans. Our public libraries' catalog shows 1,329 cookbooks that we own communally, and with 5,000 new cookbooks published annually, more are on the way. Dallas Cowboy coach Bill Parcells once noted that whoever's being asked to cook the dinner (i.e. "lead the team") ought to be able to buy the groceries (i.e. "assemble the team to be led"). Interestingly, shopping lists exist that are far older than cookbooks, and they're providing new insights into the writing of the Bible.

A recent **NYTimes.com** article by Isabel Kershner describes the archeological findings of 100 "ostracons," ink writing on pieces of pottery, that listed supplies needed at a pre-Roman Judean fortress shortly before the Babylonians conquered that land in 587 BCE. A typical ostracon read, "To Eliaship: And now, give the Kittiyim (Greek mercenaries) 3 baths of wine, and write the name of the day." Another mentioned "Add a full homer of wine, bring tomorrow; don't be late. And if there is vinegar, give it to them." For the record, **OxfordBiblicalStudies.com** says the liquid measure "bath" equaled 6.073 gallons, while "homers," a dry measure equaled 6.524 bushels.

Kershner described how Tel Aviv University's research has "combined archeology, Jewish history, and applied mathematics, and involved computerized image processing, and the development of an algorithm to distinguish between the various authors issuing commands." They were able to determine that "even soldiers in the lower ranks of the Judahite army, it appears, could read and write… And they wrote well, with hardly any mistakes." Scholars previously thought that the literacy rate in Judah was too low prior to the 586 BCE invasion to compile the Old Testament, but now they're having to reconsider.

Medical recipes also relate to today's cookbook theme. In 2013 a German specialist on ancient Syria named Kessel was studying the oldest known copy of "On the Mixtures and Powers of Drugs," an important medical book written by the Greek physician Galen of Pergamon around 200 CE and now owned by a wealthy Baltimore collector. The book was incomplete, but Kessel realized he'd recently seen one of the missing pages at a Harvard University library. The Baltimore copy of Galen's book was a "palimpsest," which is defined by Macmillan Dictionary as "a very old document that writing was removed from and the surface written on again."

Parchment is stretched animal skin, usually from sheep, and it's easy to scrape off the thick, handlettered ink used by ancient scribes, thereby recycling the pages, and in this instance hymns replaced Galen's recipes. Fortunately, modern technology recaptured the old lettering, and valuable insights into ancient medicine are being regained. The Harvard page was found in a catalog from the world's oldest continually operating library, located at the Sacred and Imperial Monastery of the God-Trodden Mount of Sinai.

Cookbooks hit their stride in the 1800s. English food writers led the evolution of modern cookbooks, according to the library's copy of "Encyclopedia of Food and Culture," and two cookbooks, "Plain Cooking for the Working Classes" (1852) and "Book of the Table" (1877) stood out in their opposing approaches. The former's author was Queen Victoria's personal chef, Charles Elme Francatelli, who "displayed compassion for women who fed their families on limited expenditures and who worked and baked at archaic hearths." Book of the Table "asserted that talent for cookery was a matter of soul," and with an author named Eneas Sweetbread Dallas, it's unsurprising that the "overbearing rhetoric bolstered the image of the chef as an artiste who functioned above the plane of the ordinary kitchen worker."

Public libraries have resources all classes need and use. The recipe for a successful library is simple: compile and organize a world of information, fold in a staff committed to public service, and add curiosity.

Khipus, Goldfish, and Memorable Mimosas

....

Khipus, knotted string records, were the data collection technology preferred by Incan royal administrators 500 years ago. A NYTimes article from last January reported that, for the first time, a collection of ancient khipus were discovered where they were actually used: in an agricultural storehouse 100 miles south of modern Lima. "Khipus are made of a series of cotton or wool strings hanging from a main cord," and are more complex than you might suppose. "Each string may have several knots, with the type and location of the knot conveying meaning. The color of the strands used to make the string and the way the strands are twisted together may also be part of the khipus' system of storing and relaying information."

But are khipus really writing? Although they've "long had a basic understanding of the numerical system incorporated in the khipus…researchers have been unable to identify the meaning of any nonnumerical signifiers." The storehouse where these recently discovered khipus were found was a staging area for troops preparing to invade southern Peru. Since the average ancient Peruvian diet has been determined, it's hoped that by comparing the khipus with crops stored nearby, the mysterious Inca knotting code may start to be unraveled, so to speak.

Mankind has always struggled with remembering, and some of us more than others. When I recently encountered another NYTimes article titled "An Ancient and Proven Way to Improve

Memorization," I read on. It described a book anonymously written in 80 BCE, "Rhetorica ad Herennium", the oldest book ever
written on rhetoric, and, among many other subjects, it "teaches
the 'method of the loci,' also known as 'the memory palace.' As
its names suggest, the approach involves associating the ideas or
objects to be memorized with memorable scenes imagined to be at
well-known locations ('loci'), like one's house ('palace') or along a
familiar walking route... Before books were common, the method
of loci helped lawyers and others retain and recall information necessary for their jobs."

All well and good, but our attention spans are dropping so rapidly that concentrating long enough to construct memory palaces
might be beyond us. According to **NetworkWorld.com**, "If you
use multiple digital devices, then you may have a shorter attention
span than a goldfish." They cite a Microsoft study that found that
the "average human attention span in 2000 was 12 seconds, but by
2013 it was only 8 seconds (1 second shorter than a goldfish)... The
research found that 'overall, digital lifestyles have a negative impact
on prolonged focus.' Multi-screening behavior, media consump-
tion, social media usage, and technology adoption rate were listed
as the top factors that impact attention span and the ability to stay
focused on a single task."

Getting a good night's sleep is a good place to start improving
your memory. **IFLScience.com** reported on a recent study out of
the University of California, Riverside that found that although
humans and animals "decouple" their brains from sensory input
during sleep, parts of their sleeping brains remain busy taking information stored in the hippocampus and transferring it to long-term
memory in the cortex. In a related study from Britain's Lancaster
University, researcher Padraic Monaghan wrote, "We now know
that sleep has profound implications for lots of human tasks." Sleep
improves memory, helps consolidate information, improves the
quality of the stored information, and has "a positive effect on
problem solving."

The saying "dumb as a stump" must be reconsidered in light of evidence from the University of Western Australia that plants have memory, too. They tested the "touch-me-not" mimosa, that folds its slender leaves when touched, by dropping it onto a foam-lined surface from a nonfatal height. "Mimosas subjected to a single drop quickly closed their leaves," but when they were repeatedly dropped they stopped closing. When retested a month later, "the plants not only remembered that the stimulus was harmless, but opened their leaves more widely, showing that they had adapted to their new environment."

If plants can do it, so can we. A poor memory's no excuse for forgetting to promptly return the library books, DVDs and the other materials we borrow before the librarians have to track us down with reminders. We enjoy the friendliest of libraries, but as James Howell pointed out, "The creditor hath a better memory than the debtor."

Flirting, Swearing, and Classy Curses

A chapter intriguingly titled "Conversation and Flirtation" immediately piqued my interest in reading "From the Ballroom to Hell: Grace and Folly in Nineteenth Century Dance," a book recommended by one of my Osher Lifelong Learning professors. It listed the various signals young people employed back then using their handkerchiefs, fans, gloves, and parasols. Biting one's glove tips, for example, meant "I wish to be rid of you very soon," while carefully folding them meant "Get rid of your company." Drawing them halfway onto the left hand meant "Indifference," but leaving just the left thumb exposed meant "Do you love me?," and turning them inside out meant "I hate you."

Placing one's handkerchief over the eyes implied "You are so cruel," placing it over the right ear was "How you have changed," and twisting it in the left hand meant, "I wish to be rid of you." Careful with the bumbershoot! Carrying it elevated in the left hand meant "Desiring acquaintance," but high in the other hand meant "You are too willing." Using them as fans meant "Introduce me to your company," and putting the handle to one's lips meant, "Kiss me."

This was an era of gentler—as well as veiled—expletives, in polite society. Over time a number of less offensive oaths have been present in English, like "humbug!," "blimey!," "God's teeth!," and "horsefeathers!" "Dag nabbit!," was one of my father's kinder expressions, and my mom's strongest oath was her seldom used but feared, "fiddlededee!" Apparently the fiddledeedee's been around since the 1400s, but, according to the Oxford English Dictionary, not used in print until 1784 when Boswell quoted Samuel "Dictionary" Johnson saying "Fiddlededee, my dear."

I admire cursing that's clean and creative, like "cork-sucking ice hole," "son of a seacook," or "holy Chinese breakfast." But sometimes terms are offensive because of their linguistic origin. A recent **NYTimes.com** article titled "Inshallah is for Everyone" is a case in point. Though "Inshallah" literally means, "If god wills it," the article's point was that sometimes saying "Inshallah is the Arabic version of 'fuggedaboudit.' It's similar to how the British use the word 'brilliant' to both praise and passive-aggressively deride everything and everyone. It transports both the speaker and the listener to a fantastical place where promises, dreams, and realistic goals are replaced by delusional hope and earnest yearning... Boy: 'Father, will we go to Toys R Us later today?' Father: 'Yes. Inshallah.' Translation: "There's no way we're going... I'm exhausted... Here, play with this staple remover."

Donald Trump has few compunctions about verbally offending others. In Jonathan Green's online article, "A Lexicographer Explains the Sneaky Agenda Behind Trump's Dirty Mouth," he says "While breaking linguistic taboos can indeed be a means of seriously challenging the stuffy status quo, a closer look at Trump's use of foul language makes it clear he has other motivations...his use of vulgar language is about winning friends and influencing people, while strategically alienating others... Trump, self-appointed man of the people, is trying through his unrestrained manner of speech to position himself as 'us,' not 'them.'"

Few humans have ever sworn as beautifully as Shakespeare, with lines like "Thine face is not worth sunburning," and "You scullion! You rampallion! You fustilarian! I'll tickle your catastrophe!" For the record, a "rampallion" is "a mean wretch," and "fustilarians" were "lowly persons." To honor Shakespeare's birth and death anniversary, I give you Aryeh Cohen-Wade's take on Donald Trump playing Hamlet. "Listen—to be, not to be, this is a tough question, O.K.? Very tough. A lot of people come up to me and ask, 'Donald, what's more noble? Getting hit every day with the slings, the bows, the arrows, the sea of troubles—or just giving up?' I mean, smart people, the best Ivy League schools. "But I say to them, 'Have you ever thought that we don't know—we don't know—what dreams may come? Have you ever thought about that?' Ay-yi-yi—there's the rub!"

Bone up on your cursing at the library, where you'll find "Holy Sh★t: A Brief History of Swearing," and other disturbing information. For if you aren't offended by something in your public library, then the librarians aren't doing their jobs of representing all legal tastes and presenting all points of view.

Flowers, Fireflies, and Frequentives

....

A recent visit to central Texas revealed that sensible rains have finally returned there after a half-decade of severe drought. The hills were green, the wild flowers still blooming, and, at dusk, lightning bugs, AKA fireflies, abounded. According to **KUT.org**, a Texas A&M entomologist named Wizzie Brown says past and present rains are key. We're "not talking about the rain this year… it takes time for a firefly to grow. They need a wet spring to lay a bunch of eggs. Then the larvae need moisture as they grow underground for at least a year before emerging."

When it comes to dictionaries, the American Heritage Unabridged Dictionary remains my personal favorite, not least because of the mini-essays interspersed through that enlarge upon interesting words. The "firefly" entry led to a "Regional Note" under "lightning bug," where I read that, "Although *firefly* remains the literary and formal word, *lightning bug* is the term used by the majority of Americans… Nearly 80 percent of those interviewed for the Dictionary of American Regional English volunteered *lightning bug*, while not quite 30 percent said *firefly*, including those who said both)."

"It's time to make love, douse the glim; The fireflies twinkle and dim," wrote Conrad Aiken. The term "twinkle" is what's known in grammar circles as a "frequentative," an adjective that expresses "frequent repetition or intensity of action," often by adding "-le". In Old English to *twincan* meant "to wink, blink," and its frequentative, *twinclian*, meant to "twinkle." Other common frequentatives include *gamble* (game), *sparkle* (spark), and *gruntle*.

"The first sense of *gruntle* was of a repeated grunt," **WorldWideWords.org** said, "especially the noise that pigs make in company... *Gruntle* appeared in the fifteenth century; by the end of the next century it had begun to be used to mean grumbling or complaining." Add an intensifier, like *dis*, to the frequentative "gruntle", and you have the unsatisfied *disgruntled,* whose opposite should logically be "happy, contented." For instance, P.G. Wodehouse's perfect fictional butler, Jeeves, waited on a perfect idiot named Bertie Wooster, who said of his servant, "He spoke with a certain what-is-it in his voice, and I could see that, if not actually disgruntled, he was far from being gruntled."

Gruntle is an "unpaired word," a word created by taking away part of it. Some unpaired words are real words anyway. *Effable* means "capable of being expressed," for example, *scrutible* means "capable of being understood," and *peccable* means "imperfect, flawed." An example of the latter is from a London Times article by Mark Dapin titled "Lost in France": "We picked up a Peugeot 406 automatic at Toulouse airport. I approached the glossy woman at the airport desk and announced in extremely peccable French: 'The car is here, brothel-owning lady, for us.'" During a recent trip to France, I distributed my retirement calling card far and wide which happily announced that I'm a "rogue librarian." A kindly Frenchman eventually enlightened me that in France a *library* is "a bookstore," and a *rogue* is a very naughty fellow, indeed, so to my new French friends I was claiming to be XXX bookstore operator.

Perhaps *kamishibai's* behind my latest word-fixation. Kamishibai means "paper-theater" in Japan, where storytellers once bicycled from town to town with a miniature stage and case of candy strapped to the back. The storyteller/candyman used illustrated scrolls or sheets in the stage to tell long, fanciful stories, making sure the purchasers of the sweets he vended sat up front. According to

Kamishibai.com, "Kamishibai is, if anything, poor man's theater, and it flourished during a time when Japan experienced extreme financial hardship... By the 1950s and the advent of television, kamishibai had become so popular that television was initially referred to as *denki kamishibai,* or 'electric kamishibai.'"

Like so much in life, I encountered kamishibai in a book, *Birdsong,* by James Sturm. It's part of the excellent TOON Book series, "the first high-quality comics designed for children ages three and up... Each TOON book has been vetted by educators to ensure that the language and the narratives will nurture young minds." They're fun, informative, and very-well made, and our library has scads of them. They're perfect for our library's "On Your Mark, Get Set... READ!" summer reading program for ages two and up. It's an excellent way to immerse your child in words. Like John Ray said, "Good words cool more than cold water."

Obnubilate Zinio, Y'all

The words from **TheAtlantic.com** fell on my ears like manna in the desert: "How y'all doing? A greeting as Southern as a bowl of grits, it rolls off the tongue in a single open-mouth utterance. Sweeter than honey, and often saturated with hidden meaning, it can open up a dialogue with a roomful of strangers with ease. Part of that ease hinges on the incredible versatility of the phrase's most important words. 'Y'all,' that strange regional and ethnic conjunction, offers a simplicity to speech that can't be found elsewhere. It is a magnificently elegant linguistic creation."

Another pro-y'all article, "American Needs Y'all," written by Vann Newkirk II, goes on to note there's "no distinct second-person plural pronouns in modern standard English." Other languages have ways of referring to multiple other people, Newkirk said, such as "vosotros" in Spanish and "nyinyi" in Swahili, but "modern English requires that 'you' be jury-rigged in order to fulfill its true plural purpose." In King James' day "ye" filled the bill, but it has long since become obsolete. The Brits say "you lot," while some Americans also employ "youse," "you-uns," and "yinz."

The popularity of "you guys" is falling in our "era of increased scrutiny and consideration over the gender of pronouns... Plus, it's just a damn clunky way to speak." Speaking of which, old memories were dredged up by reading a **NYTimes.com** article by Patricia Cohen titled "At the World Bank, a Shortage of Concrete Language." Cohen described how the Stanford University Literary

Lab analyzed 65 years of the World Bank's publications and "found a sharp decline in factual precision, replaced by what the researchers called management discourse, a bureaucratic gobbledygook whose meaning is hard to decipher... The result is titled 'Bankspeak,' a play on doublespeak, referring to language that is intentionally ambiguous, meant to obscure or confuse."

This pattern of obscurity increased sharply 20 years ago. Verbs were increasingly used as nouns, "the use of adverbs that refer to a particular time frame (such as 'now,' 'recently,' 'or 'later') declined by more than 50%. Past tense verbs grew rarer, while jargon and acronyms proliferated."

I witnessed early vestiges of Bankspeak's development first-hand during a stint at the U.S. State Department 40 years ago that included free access to the World Bank library, as well as libraries at the CIA, Treasury, Census Bureau, and even a coveted stackpass to the Library of Congress. It was at the World Bank Library that I found some articles that were questioning the decline in the way information was being communicated in ever-finer definitions and ever-vaguer terminology.

The Romans had a word for this: "obnubilate," or "make less visible or clear." **WorldWideWords.org** guru Anu Garg described obnubilate...as high-flown a Latinate word as the clouds it figuratively evokes—it comes from 'nubes,' a cloud." The folks at the Thesaurus Linguae Latinae, a monumentally detailed Latin Dictionary, would confirm that, but they skipped the "N" volume of their ultimate Latin dictionary "because it has so many long words," according to an online article by Byrd Pinkerton. Work is proceeding on the "N" and "R" volumes simultaneously, which ought to take them the rest of the decade. Not bad, considering they've been at it since 1894.

Another sort of dictionary has been created by the makers of the "Infant Cries Translator" app. Over the past two years researchers at the National Taiwan University Hospital Yunlin "have compiled 200,000 different sounds from 100 newborns and uploaded them to create a massive online database. The Infant Cries Translator can differentiate four different types of baby crying, including hunger, the diaper getting wet, sleepy, and pain, and it claims a 92% accuracy rate for babies under two weeks old, 85% at two months, and 77% after four months.

I read about this new app in "News of the Weird," a feature in Funny Times Magazine, which I can borrow from the public library. It's one of some 550 print magazine subscriptions at our library, along with 80 more digital magazines available through the library's free online Zinio service. Moreover, these days some magazines formerly only available in print, like PC Mag and MacWorld, can only be had now digitally.

"Cabin Life," "Birding," "The Atlantic," and scads of other worthy publications can be downloaded through Zinio, but to get a copy of "Southern Living," you'll need to visit your library, where I hope to see all y'all.

Gobblefunk, Gold Cards, and Blind Boy Groot

Roald Dahl, creator of Willie Wonka and "James and the Giant Peach," liked naming things so much that the Oxford Roald Dahl Dictionary will soon be published. He coined over 500 words, collectively termed "gobblefunk" ('if you gobblefunk with words, you play around with them and invent new words or meanings'). They're among the 8,000 amusing words he utilized "as a method of keeping children engaged in books," according to a recent Public Radio International article by Joshua Kelly. Other examples of Dahl's coinages include "phizzwizard" (defined as "a good dream that leaves you feeling happy when you wake up"), and "troggle-humper" ("one of the very worst nightmares you can have").

Rock groups adore intriguing and unusual band names. ? and the Mysterians, whose one hit was "96 Tears," began performing as "the Mysterians and XYZ?" Their "eccentric front man, Rudy Martinez, legally changed his named to the question mark symbol," and thereafter he fronted their band name, according to "Rock Name Band Origins," a fun book I encountered at our public library,

The Beach Boys tried performing as Kenny and the Cadets, Carl and the Passions, and even the Pendletones, named after the Pendleton shirts then favored by surfers. And Creedence Clearwater Revival came from the first name of a guy named Credence Nuball, which was combined with part of an Olympia Beer ad and a reference to the band's return to "the basic simplicity of rock and roll."

In "On Names," Michel Montaigne wrote, "it is a good thing to have a good name (meaning renown or reputation); but it is also a real advantage to have a fine one which is easy to pronounce and to remember." However, a surprising number of countries have strict naming laws that limit parents' choices. Sweden's 1982 Naming Law, originally intended to prohibit non-nobles from adopting titled monikers, now has been extended to read, "First names shall not be approved if they can cause offense or can be supposed to cause discomfort for the one using it." Metallica, Superman, Elvis, and Ikea have all been rejected, along with Brfxxccxxmnpcccclllmmnprxvclmnckssqlbb11116 (pronounced Albin), the latter being a name submitted by parents opposed to the Naming Law. Their next suggestion, "A" (also pronounced Albin), was shot down as well.

Naming a baby "Lego" is fine, though, as it also is in Germany, another strict naming country. Names must be conjugatible in Iceland and contain only letters from the Icelandic alphabet. So Bambi is OK, but Harriet (can't conjugate) and Duncan (no "C" in Icelandic), aren't. And I don't know what's in the parental water in New Zealand, whose non-offensive naming laws rejected the baby names Stallion, Yeah Detroit, Sex Fruit, Satan and Adolph Hitler, but Violence, Midnight Chardonnay, and Number 16 Bus Shelter were all approved.

While we're at it, "42 of the Best Least Popular Baby Names from 100 Years Ago," a **MentalFloss.com** article by Akira Okrent, said that adherents of the current craze for unusual baby names should check the Social Security Administration's records for some doozies. The top 1,000 names from 1916 included General (ranked 775th least popular), Major (499), Loyal (696), and Vernal (914) for boys, and Pinkie (749), Dimple (895), Versie (914), and Wava (992) for girls.

Another library reference book, "Musical AKAs: Assumed Names and Sobriquets of Composers, Songwriters, Librettists, Hymnists, and Writers on Music," lists names popular musicians have utilized. For instance, Robert Allen Zimmerman, AKA Bob Dylan (and Dillon and Dillion), also performed as Roosevelt Gook, Jack Frost, Lucky Wilbury, and Blind Boy Groot. But Zimmerman can't compete with Daniel DeFoe, author of "Robinson Crusoe" and the penname champ.

According to **RegistryOfPseudonyms.com**, his real name was "Foe," but to distinguish Daniel from his father James, "D. Foe" became "DeFoe." He was incredibly prolific, writing books, pamphlets, poems, and diatribes under 198 pen names, many of which would make great rock band names, like Count Kidney Face, Anti-Bubbler, Sir Foppling Tittle Tattle, and Urgentissimus.

I like being called a "Gold Card patron." Support the Fairbanks Library Foundation with a $50 annual donation, and you'll receive a lovely golden card, attesting to your love of books and libraries. But the regular library card's pretty, too, and as Helen Hunt Jackson noted, "Bee to the blossom, moth to the flame; Each to his passion; what's in a name?"

Synesthesia, Misophonia, and Argle-Bargle

....

A number of articles about synesthesia have cropped up lately. Reading Vladimir Nabokov's wonderful memoir, "Speak Memory," revealed his personal synesthesia manifestation: seeing letters as particular colors. "V is a kind of pale, transparent pink," Nabokov said, "technically, quartz pink...the N, on the other hand, is a greyish-yellowish oatmeal color."

Synesthesia occurs in about 1% of the population who otherwise can otherwise "lead normal, healthy lives except that they experience additional sensations to sensory stimuli, viz. colors or tastes for words, touch for sounds, and so on." It "arises when an increased number of nerve fibers interconnect discrete regions of the brain," according to "Some Rules of Language Are Wired in the Brain," a **ScientificAmerican.com** article. For example, James Wannerton, a British synethete, finds that words and names come with taste sensations, presumably arising "from a cross-talk between word processing and taste centers of his brain."

The most common manifestations of synesthesia are sensing colors when they hear music, or see numbers in color, as in the number 3 appearing blue, 4 green, etc. A possibly related condition, misophonia, affects people who become painfully annoyed by certain sounds. In "Please Stop Making That Noise," a **NYTimes.com** article, Barron Lerner, M.D. wrote that someone chewing popcorn with an open mouth is truly insufferable. "I have misophonia, a condition with which certain sounds can drive someone into a burst of rage or disgust."

Misophonia, or "hatred of sound," was coined by Professors Margaret and Pawel Jastreboff of Emory University in 2002. A 2013 University of Amsterdam study described "the most common irritants as eating sounds, including lip-smacking and swallowing; breathing sounds, such as nostril noises and sneezing; and hand sounds, such as typing and pen clicking... Researchers are only beginning to understand the science behind misophonia, but early data suggests a hyperconnectivity between the auditory system and the limbic system, a part of the brain responsible for generating emotions." The five most irritating sounds are, in ascending order, knuckle cracking, nail clipping, sniffling, gum chewing, and, worst of all, slurping.

Some poor souls find certain words deeply repellent, a condition known as "word aversion." Some researchers are theorizing that word aversion is related to synesthesia, but others propose that words associated with certain concepts, especially body functions, are what's actually behind word aversion. The most widely despised word appears to be "moist." Oberlin College researcher Paul Thibodeau wrote that "moist" is "not a taboo word, it's not profanity, but it elicits this very visceral disgust reaction in many people." However, Thibodeau found that "words that sound similar—including hoist, foist, and rejoiced—did not put off participants the same way, suggesting that aversion to the word was not based on the way it sounds. But people who were bothered by moist also found that words for bodily fluids—vomit, puke, and phlegm—largely struck a nerve."

A readers' survey conducted by the NYTimes also found that disgust extended to words describing body parts as well, and "words describing various sorts of vocalizations were mentioned so frequently that they could be cataloged in alphabetical order. The Gs alone would include the words gulp, gargle, grunt, groan, and gasp." One reader combined a number of the most despised terms into a single sentence, "I read this after stroking my moist slacks to remove phlegm that must have come from a crevice on the luggage

of my Ford Probe." There are certainly other word aversion categories; the woman I live with, for instance, abhors words associated
with food, like "dollop" and "creamy."

Fortunately there are some happy words out there, especially
reduplicatives, which **OxfordDictionaries.com** defines as repeat-
ing a syllable or other linguistic element exactly or with a slight
change. Examples include the relatively recent "argle-bargle"
(a vigorous discussion or dispute) from 1872 which stems from
"argle," an obsolete synonym for "argue." There are "hugger-mug-
ger" (secret, confused) from 1529, and don't forget 1668's "hoity-
toity" (haughty, pretentious), which comes from "hoit," an old
word meaning "to romp." And 1440 saw the first printed mention
of both "tussie-mussie" (a small bouquet of flowers) and "hurly-
burly" (disorder, confusion).

Many of my favorite words come from our library: "no overdue
fines," "open stacks," "free," "storehouse of knowledge," and, best
of all, "books."

Fine, Criticism, and Ms. Mutch

Constructive criticism can be helpful, or hurtful, depending on how and when it's delivered. For example, Donna Haraway's 1991 book titled "Primate Visions" was reviewed rather harshly by anthropologist Matt Cartmill in the International Journal of Primatology. "This is a book that systematically distorts and selects historical evidence," Cartmill opined, "but that is not a criticism, because its author thinks that all interpretations are biased, and she regards it as her duty to pick and choose her facts to favor her own brand of politics... This is a book that clatters around in a dark closet of irrelevancies for 450 pages before it bumps accidentally into its index and stops."

There are more constructive ways to say things like that. That's the focus of "Is This the Right Moment?," a recent online article by Anne Curzan about correcting others' grammatical errors. "Correcting someone's language can feel like criticism even when it's not meant that way...we should realize that doing so can be loaded." Curzan recommends first considering, "Will this person really benefit from having you call out this bit of language?," and "is this a good moment? If so, then go ahead—and do it kindly. If not, if the speech will make you feel smart but not really help the other person, then consider keeping the correction in your head."

Bruised feelings can be exacerbated when one's supposed errors stem from the upwelling of unusual grammar arising from social media rather than forgetting what Mrs. Strickland taught us in

5th grade English. Some of us prefer adhering to Mrs. Strickland's rules rather than Twitter's, and don't appreciate having beliefs like "periods are passé" foisted upon us. Last month the NYTimes ran "Period. Full Stop. Point. Whatever it's Called, It's Going Out of Style," an article by Dan Bilefsky that maintained that the 140-character limit imposed on tweets is causing a general decline in the use of punctuation. It quotes David Crystal, a British author of "more than 100 books on language," who asked "In an instant message, it is pretty obvious a sentence has come to an end...so why use it?"

In social media, Crystal said, "the period is being deployed as a weapon to show irony, syntactic snark, insincerity, even aggression." Nowadays, after making an elaborate meal and then being stood up, for instance, "you are best advised to include a period when you respond "Fine." to show annoyance. "Fine" or "Fine!," in contrast, could denote acquiescence or blithe acceptance. The period now has an emotional charge and has become an emoticon of sorts."

This reasoning smacks of the same smug self-assurance of the 1990s futurists who foretold the eminent death of print books and libraries, since soon everyone would own an inexpensive computer and through it have free access to every scrap of information known to mankind. Today more print books are being published than ever before, and society's need for the root functions of libraries—collecting information, organizing it and getting it to users—remains unchanged, just as it has for the last 5,000 years.

I predict that periods will continue to be utilized, because they facilitate readers' comprehension, like spaces in between words, paragraphs, standardized spelling, and common sense grammar. Nonetheless, I don't go along with grammatical persnicketiness, because sometimes effective communications requires bending those rules. And I admire the great noir writer Raymond Chandler's letter, gently delivered as a poem he wrote to his publisher's overbearing proofreader, one Margaret Mutch, who disapproved of Chandler's penchant for splitting infinitives. His lengthy letter includes, "A lot of my style (so-called) is vile For I learned to write in a bar. The marriage of thought to words was wrought With many a strong sidecar. A lot of my stuff is extremely rough, For I had no maiden aunts. O dear Miss Mutch, leave go your clutch On Noah Webster's pants! The grammarian will, when the poet lies still, Instruct him in how to sing. The rules are clean: they are right, I ween, But where do they make the thing?… O leave us dance on the dead romance Of the small but clear footnote. The infinitive with my fresh-honed shiv I will split from heel to throat."

Songs, Styles, and Rackslappers

Frank Sinatra was known for the finely stylized phrasing of his songs, and Sammy Cahn was his favorite lyricist. Cahn hit the big time in 1937 when he re-wrote in English the words to a Yiddish tune called "Bei Mir Bist Du Schon." A singing trio called the Andrews Sisters who'd just arrived in the Big Apple heard it at his apartment, asked to record it, and they all soon became wealthy and famous. Cahn often wrote special lyrics for particular singers, like "Three Coins in the Fountain" for the most particular of all: Sinatra.

Sinatra refused to appear in the MGM musical "Anchors Away" unless Cahn wrote the music's words, and Cahn was still at it when Old Blue Eyes starred in the Rat Pack classic, "Robin and the 7 Hoods." In it he wrote a forgettable duet for Sinatra and Dean Martin called "Style": "You've either got or you haven't got style. If you got it, you stand out a mile. A flower's not a flower if it's wilted. A hat's not a hat 'til it's tilted. You either got or your haven't got class. How it draws the applause from the masses!"

Raymond Queneau knew something about style, too. The library's Dictionary of Literary Biography database rated Queneau "one of the most amusing and versatile French writers of the twentieth century. He was a poet, novelist, critic, editor, playwright, filmmaker, philosopher, mathematician, and even a painter." Nonetheless, Queneau was always suspicious of fads and fashions and "kept his distance from literary movements." He was interested in style, however. In 1958 Queneau published "Exercises in Style" in which he "presents an insignificant incident... This incident is recounted in ninety-nine different ways or styles, each one varying the arrangement of events and choice of diction, tone, and emphasis. One such style is termed metaphoric, another tactile, still others exclamatory and vulgar...his purpose is to rid literature of its rusty, crusty conventions."

Unfortunately, our library doesn't own that book, but the librarians can borrow it for you from a library that has it through the wonderful interlibrary loan program. Our library loans books that are needed by other libraries' patrons, and in return, we can borrow books from thousands of other libraries, thereby making almost any book obtainable, free of charge.

Our library owns a similar, and, in my opinions, better, book: Matt Madden's "99 Ways to Tell a Story: Exercises in Style." Like Queneau, Madden takes a simple story—a man gets up from his computer workstation and walks into another room to get something from the fridge, another person asks him the time, and then he can't remember what he was looking for—but Madden does it through the medium of graphic literature, AKA "comics." A review of "99 Ways" by Scott Pack in another library database, Literature Resource Center, observed that "By giving us a comic book version, Madden is able to be more original, more surreal, and more amusing than Queneau." For example, one of the versions of the story is told from the perspective of the refrigerator, and another is done as a map.

Having read both books, I can attest that Queneau's is initially intriguing, but ultimately rather forced, while Madden's is more inventive, entertaining, and, compelling. By combining words with illustrations in a sequential manner, many more permutations to storytelling are possible. Publisher's Weekly observed in its starred review of Madden's book, "A new discovery awaits the reader on every page...new elements are introduced and removed: different characters, more panels, fewer close-ups, flashbacks, text-only, or a focus on sound or color effects... Favorites include a how-to on building a comic, a palindromic story that reads the same backward and forward, and a calligram (with text formed into a question mark shape).

Madden's book is so rich, it's hard to select a favorite style. Styles are forever transitory and mutable, and it's nice to know there are many to choose from. But as Molly Ivins noted, "The trouble is, once one has managed to achieve a style that indicates one's status group and expresses one's personality, then a whole herd of Bloomingdale's rack-slappers comes along and copies it, and then one has to start all over."

Obscure Sorrows, Crosswords, and Amyloids

A child of mine recently passed along the online Dictionary of Obscure Sorrows, a collection of neologisms—newly coined words—created by John Koenig to define "emotions that do not have a descriptive term." According to Wikipedia, Koenig's neologisms "are based on his research on etymologies and meanings of used prefixes, suffixes, and word roots. The terms are often based on 'feelings of existentialism' and are meant to fill 'a hole in the language.'" A couple of examples are, "klexos: the art of dwelling in the past," and "lutalica: the part of your identity that doesn't fit into categories." Though not a particularly gloomy Gus, I identified with one of Koenig's terms, "kudoclasm: when lifelong dreams are brought down."

After working at the Texas Legislature for five years, and wallowing in political kudoclasm, I renewed its acquaintance at my first job out of library school at a corrupt West Texas public library. The library served 100,000 people, but it only purchased new books one or two days a year, when two of the librarians were flown to Dallas by a book company, wined and dined, and given a few hours to buy all the library's new books for the year from that very dealer, who sold remaindered, or leftover, books that are usually heavily discounted 50% and more. I surveyed hundreds of books that arrived at that library under the guise of new books, and found they had average copyright dates of 1904 and cost over $40, even though back then new bestsellers cost less than $15. After turning over my evidence to the county attorney, who advised me to leave town fast. I did, taking a job as director of a small public library on the other side of the state.

A more recent kudoclasm cropped up when I learned about the nefarious plagiarism of USA Today crossword-puzzle editor Timothy Parker. Last March a website focusing on polls, politics, and economics, called FiveThirtyEight, reported that "a group of eagle-eyed puzzlers, using digital tools, has uncovered a pattern of copying in the professional crossword-puzzle world." Parker was USA Today's crossword editor for 15 years until software engineer Saul Pwanson created first a database of 52,000 recent puzzles, along with a program that identified puzzles that match up with another at least 25 percent of the time.

There are often some similarities between competing puzzles. "To me," Parker said, "it's just mere coincidence." However, Pwanson found that the New York Time's puzzles had similarities with others 0.1 percent of the time, Los Angeles Times 0.3%, Wall Street Journal 0.4%, but USA had significant similarities at a 16% rate. Last May USA Today announced that neither they nor Gannet, their parent company, will publish any crosswords associated with Parker, which somewhat lightened my kudoclasm.

Crosswords can reveal much about us. NYTimes contributor Charles Kurzman recently suspected that Americans are becoming "more parochial than our grandparents' generation," so he downloaded all the Times' crosswords from between 1942-2015 and "created an algorithm to search all 2,092,375 pairs of clues and answers for foreign language words and place names outside the United States." He found "the puzzle today uses one-third fewer international references than in its peak in 1943," something of a surprise in this age of globalization.

Nonetheless, working on crosswords is a valuable activity. It's true that American Crossword Puzzle champion Dan Feyer won a mere $5,000 prize for his feat, but by exerting your brain regularly with crosswords, reading deeply, and doing other mental exercises, you can stave off Alzheimer's. According to **ALZ.org**, UC Berkeley researchers used brain scans looking for an imaging agent called "Pittsburg compound B" that binds to beta-amyloid, "a toxic protein that builds up in the brains of those with Alzheimer's and is the main component of the brain plaques that characterize the disease."

They found that "the more someone engaged in mentally stimulating activities, the less buildup of beta-amyloid they were likely to have in the brain... The brains of seniors who engaged in mentally stimulating activities most often were comparable to those of young people."

The sooner in life you start exercising your brain, the Berkeley guys say, the better it will fend off beta-amyloid plaque buildup. How much is that worth? Certainly visiting your public library, that grand gymnasium for the mind. You'll find more mental stimulation there than you'll ever get through in a dozen lifetimes of TV viewing, and you'll have fun. On the other hand, morose old Koenig might say your library's got "vellichor: the strange wistfulness of used bookstores, which are somehow infused with the passage of time."

Words, Colors, and OZ

R onald Reagan was the source of "the glass is half empty or half full" line, according to the Random House Dictionary of Popular Proverbs and Sayings. However, the Dictionary of Modern Proverbs says that in 1935 the economist Sir Josiah Stamp said the difference between optimists and pessimists is, "A pessimist looks at his glass and says it is half empty, an optimist looks at it and says it is half full. Today I've chosen to emulate the president and economist and eschew my recent proclivity for discussing unpopular words, like "moist" and "unctuous," and negative words such as "plagiarism" and "kudoclasm."

So I won't dwell too long describing Pantone 448c, AKA "opaque couche" or "the world's ugliest color." The pigment was the result of the Australian government's search for the most unappealing color to use for tobacco product packaging to dissuade smokers. According to the **HouseBeautiful.com** article "It's Lovingly Described as Death" by Caroline Picard, the "sewage-tinged hue" was initially called "olive green,", but "after an urgent letter from the Australian Olive Association, they changed the nickname to "drab dark brown."

Instead of Pantone 448c, let's reflect on the positive side of our language, as in a wonderful letter written by Robert Pirosh in 1934. Pirosh was a young, unemployed copywriter who sent the following letter to every potential employer he could think of. "Dear sir, I like words. I like fat buttery words, such as ooze, turpitude, glutinous, toady. I like solemn, angular, creaky words, such as straightlaced, cantankerous, pecunious, valedictory. I like spurious, black-is-white words, such as mortician, liquidate, tonsorial, demi-monde. I like suave "V" words, such as Svengali, svelte, bravura, verve. I like crunchy, brittle, crackly words, such as splinter, grapple, jostle, crusty. I like sullen, crabbed, scowling words, such as skulk, glower, scabby, churl. I like Oh-heavens, my gracious, lands-sakes words, such as tricksy, tucker, genteel, horrid. I like elegant, flowery words, such as estivate, peregrinate, Elysium, halcyon. I like wormy, squirmy, mealy words, such as crawl, blubber, squeal, drip. I like sniggly, chuckling words, such as cowlick, gurgle, bubble and burp.

"I like the word screenwriter better than copywriter, so I decided to quit my job in a New York advertising agency and try my luck in Hollywood, but before taking the plunge I went to Europe for a year of study, contemplation, and horsing around. I have just returned and still like words. May I have a few with you?" Pirosh was hired by MGM.

Pirosh's letter is included in "Letters of Note: Correspondence Deserving of a Wider Audience," that I found at our public library. It's chock full of amazing letters, including Beethoven's posthumous letter to his brothers, who didn't know of his deafness and thought he was just being grumpy, and others from Gandhi to Hitler, Groucho Marx to Woody Allen, and Jackie Robinson to President Eisenhower. It's a big, coffee table book known in the library world as "oversized." Libraries often place their oversized, or "OZ," books at the end of the nonfiction bookstacks to allow the shelves holding smaller, more common books to be closer to each other and thereby maximize storage.

OZ books shouldn't be confused with L. Frank Baum's Oz books, but it's worth noting that "The Wonderful Wizard of Oz" is among "Bruce Springsteen's Reading List: 28 Books That Shaped His Mind and Music," along with "Moby Dick," "Leaves of Grass" by Walt Whitman, and, a personal favorite, Sarah Bakewell's "How to Live: Or A Life of Montaigne in One Question and Twenty Attempts at an Answer."

It's daunting to narrow the field of beloved, books down like that, but it's an expansive, healthy exercise nonetheless. Despite the violent ugliness that seems to swallow the world at times, there are so many wonderful things to notice if we simply ponder on it for a moment. Where and when we live is pretty marvelous, historically speaking, especially when you add the availability of free and ready sources of information, inspiration, and intellectual stimulation known as public libraries.

Why, even the embracing of ugly old Pantone 448c has caused a big drop in Australian smoking and saved countless lives. And "Beauty," as H.G. Wells noted, "is in the heart of the beholder."!

Political Women, Dog Whistles, and Lady Bird

....

"The Politics Book" popped up during a recent foray to the public library, and my old librarian's eye was attracted by the "DK" on the cover. DK stands for Dorling Kindersly, a British publisher who describes itself as "founded in London in 1974 and is now the world's leading illustrated reference publisher and part of Penguin Random House... DK publishes highly visual, photographic non-fiction for adults and children. DK produces content for consumers in over 87 countries and 62 languages." In short, they publish eye-poppingly-engaging, quick-read reference books. "How," I wondered, "could something as broad and nebulous as politics fit in the DK mold?"

So I checked it out and found that the historical overview of politics was, as some reviewers noted, distilled and simplified, but it also was made some complex topics easily digestible. There I learned about philosopher Georg Hegel's curious view on the root of slavery being the slave's obsequiousness: "If a man is a slave, his own will is responsible for his slavery," Hegel wrote, "the wrong of slavery lies at the door not of enslavers or conquerors but of the slaves and conquered themselves."

DK's overview of John Stuart Mill's philosophy, particularly his thoughts on "tyranny of the majority," revived more pleasant memories. The staffs of Texas legislators in the 1970s consisted of a secretary and an aide. As Representative "Smiling" Dave Allred's aide I was once asked to research Mill's "majority tyranny" reasoning, which I pursued in the Legislative Reference Library, a crackerjack, even elite, library dedicated to supporting research of the Texas Legislature. Like any good librarian, the library director helped me nail the answer, and a friendship ensued that led to him recommending me to library school and hiring me as his night reference librarian, thereby connecting me to a career I could embrace passionately.

Working at the Reference Library and the Legislature certainly heightened my sensitivity to political nuance, maybe even rubbing it raw. A recent Economist article, "War of Words: Women Are Judged By the Way They Speak," caught my attention. "Female politicians are easily labeled: from the battle-axe to the national mum...the way they speak, the main task of politicians everywhere, is the most important sources of their influence and the biggest potential pitfall... The pitfalls for women's political language come at every level, from tone of voice to word-choice to the topics of conversation to conversational styles... A study in 2012 showed that a bland political slogan, digitally altered to make it deeper, was more appealing to voters, no matter whether the voters were male or female."

The article cited the example of Margaret Thatcher, who "took elocution lessons in the 1970s as she prepared to become the Conservative Party's leader and ultimately prime minister. A surprisingly girlish voice from the 1960s became a commanding and much-admired tone during her premiership." In fact, "the more 'male" a woman behaves in a leadership setting, the more authority she gains." A worrisome consideration, perhaps.

More disconcerting than women having to act like men is the growing use of political "dog whistles," defined as "a coded message that appears innocuous to the general public, but that has an additional interpretation meant to appeal to the target audience." The classic example, at least from my Southern boyhood, was when politicians said they supported "states' rights." That meant they were against racial integration and for segregation. "Ghetto" meant "black part of town," and "anointed" was code for "speaking in tongues" and other Pentecostal activities.

This gets us into the realm of euphemisms, "a word or phrase used as a way of saying something without actually saying it directly." Not all euphemisms are negative, and many are useful in polite society, such as discussing body parts and functions with small children. Euphemistic dog whistles, aside, what counts in life is to be as open-minded and well-informed as possible so when important decisions loom, like electing our nation's leaders, your choices will be based on solid facts, rather than misleading or hidden messages from scoundrels intent on deception.

The very best place to get well-rounded information that you can depend upon is your public library. As Lady Bird Johnson said, "Perhaps no place in any community is so totally democratic as the town library. The only entrance requirement is interest."

Skimming, Scanning, and Illiteracy

....

The French started using the term "desperer: to be dismayed, lose hope, despair" in the 1300s, which was an especially horrible century, filled with plague, years without summers, and the 100 Years War, among other horrors. Despair comes easily these days, too, especially when they talk about the demise of paragraphs. In "Breaking Point: Is the Writing on the Wall for Paragraphs?," Guardian writer Andy Bodle wrote that the tsunami of information sweeping social media is causing online writers to use fewer words and make the words they use punchier. "Reading on a laptop screen or phone is slower and more fatiguing," Bodle wrote, "and it's harder to keep your place. The ideal online posting today is 200 words long or less, and the Associated Press requires articles to be between 300 and 500 words long, with exceptionally involved articles running up to 700 words. The average length of political soundbites in 1968 was 43 seconds; today it's less than eight.

What we know as the paragraph came along 400 years ago, but writers long before were using indents, spacing, and symbols to indicate to readers when speakers, scenes, or topics changed. The Greeks used "horizontal strokes, wedges, and hooks" in the 3rd Century BCE. They called these indicators "paragraphos: a short stroke in the margin marking a break in sense," according to the Online Etymology Dictionary. But in those days bookmakers weren't concerned with facilitating reading with trivialities like punctuation. According to E.H. Lewis' "History of the English

Paragraph (1894)," the great printer William Tyndale, the first to translate and print the Bible in English, was also the first "tolerable paragrapher."

From the 1400s to 1900 the average paragraph length was 300 words. Although the number of sentences in these paragraphs doubled in that timeframe, their length was halved. Along the way the backward capital "P" known as the "pilcrow" was used by editors to indicate when paragraphs should begin and end. As for the etymology of "pilcrow," the Oxford English Dictionary says, "the history of the word is obscure, and evidence is wanting." Still, as Bodle noted, "Paragraphs allow us to group gobbets of information together in (more or less) coherent units. A long paragraph can be a reasoned, nuanced discourse. Lots of short paragraphs create the impression of unconnected slogans, with no obvious progression."

These days, skimming and scanning is diminishing reading, that distinctly different activity. In a 2014 Washington Post article University of Texas reading researcher Andrew Dillon said, "We're spending so much time touching, pushing, linking, scrolling, and jumping through text that when we sit down with a novel, your daily habits of jumping, clicking, linking is just ingrained in you." I've certainly experienced difficulty in getting into a book because my mind keeps jumping off to other things before settling down, and I bet you've experienced something similar.

A **PRI.org** article by T.J. Raphael said "Neuroscience, in fact, has revealed that humans use different parts of the brain when reading from a piece of paper or from a screen. So the more you read on screens, the more your mind shifts towards 'non-linear' reading." Raphael quotes WNYC's Manoush Zomorodi, editor of "New Tech City": "They call it a 'bi-literate' brain. The problem is that many of us have adapted to reading online just too well. And if you don't use the deep reading part of your brain, you lose the deep reading part of your brain."

The effects of skimming and scanning are more pronounced on youngsters, who are potentially facing lives of functional illiteracy.

According to a frightening article from **www.BeginToRead.
com/research/literacystatistics.html,** "two-thirds of students
who cannot read proficiently by the end of the fourth grade will
end up in jail or on welfare...85% of all juveniles who interface
with the juvenile court system are functionally illiterate...over 70%
of inmates in America's prisons cannot read above a fourth grade
level," and so on.

Yet reading keeps being marginalized into academic choredom
instead of being promoted as something to embrace and enjoy. I'd
despair if it weren't for our wonderful local librarians doing their
level best to make reading fun. As Will Rogers, said, "There are
three kinds of men. The one that learns by reading. The few who
learn by observation. The rest of them have to pee on the electric
fence for themselves."

Deep Reading, Lizard Feet, and Touch Cookies

....

Those immersed in the reading life know an engrossing dance of words and concepts can induced by good writing, and they're all too aware of how grating bad writing can be, like when Dorothy Parker wrote in a book review, "There have been times when her sedulously tortuous style, her one-word sentences, and her curiously compounded adjectives, drive me into an irritation that is only to be relieved by kicking and screaming." Non-book reviewers can always simply stop reading annoying books. But with authors as regularly delightful as Ms. Parker, the prose is worth savoring enough to look up unfamiliar words, like "sedulous: showing dedication and diligence," from the Latin "sedulus: painstaking, zealous."

Patrick O'Brian is another author whose prose is always worth fully understanding. In his historical novel "The Truelove," readers encounter a rough reception on board a wooden sailing ship in which were served "some little ferrinaceous objects fresh from the galley." I suspected O'Brian was implying the little objects were hard, but according to the American Heritage Dictionary (AHD), "ferrinaceous" means "made from, rich in, or consisting of starch," from the word "farina," a grain. Coincidentally, a political limerick I encountered recently included the term, "farraginous," which the AHD defined as "composed of a variety of substances," from the Latin "farrago: medley, hodgepodge, mixed grains for animal feed."

Serious readers enjoy encountering medleys and hodgepodges of unusual and useful words. Oiling an old baseball glove a few weeks ago led to wondering about the origin of neat's foot oil. Neat's foot oil's been supplanted by more sophisticated concoctions these days, but in my boyhood it was the ointment of choice for glove limbering. Since then I've harbored obscure suspicions that neats were akin to newts or lizards and that thousands of tiny feet were being sacrificed on the altar of suppleness.

When I learned that 5.1 million baseball gloves were sold in the U.S. in 2010, these worrisome thoughts arose anew, but my trusty AHD assured me that "neat" is an archaic term for "a cow or other domestic bovine animal," and neat's foot oil is "a light yellow oil obtained from the feet and shinbones of cattle, used chiefly to dress leather." Relieved, I went on to learn from the Online Etymology Dictionary that "neat" has several competing origins, with one coming from the Latin "nitidus: well-favored, elegant, trim." The bovine use of the word comes from the Proto-Germanic term, "nautum: thing of value." In the 1540s "neat" meant "clean, free from dirt," and by the 1570s it also meant "unadulterated, or straight" as in "I'll have my whiskey neat, barkeep." "Neat" came to slangishly mean "very good" in 1934; "neato," as in "neato torpedo!" was first recorded in 1968.

Deep reading widely often encompasses exposure to new, amazingly precise words, and some widely-read authors with strong vocabularies are incredibly amusing, if you get their gist. Whole websites have been dedicated to the interesting words hilariously employed by master humorist P.G. Wodehouse, such as "embrocation" (pain-relieving liquid rubbed on the body), and "gumboil" (swelling in the mouth near an abscess).

Don't bother guessing how many verbal gems are lost to speed readers employing skimming and scanning rather than deep, fully immersed reading. As a devotee of scanning library and bookstore shelves, known in bibliographic circles as "browsing," I appreciate searching quickly for something that I expect to be close by, but there are times when I want to examine things in depth. Training one's brain to focus intently on writing, or "deep reading," creates the opportunity to glimpse the human experience through other eyes.

Consider the concept of "poetic diction" created by British philosopher and author Owen Barfield. A friend recently loaned me a copy of Barfield's book, "Poetic Diction," in which he defined poetic diction as, "When words are selected and arranged in such a way that their meaning either arouses, or is obviously intended to arouse, aesthetic imagination." Great authors move our imaginations to new realms outside our normal existence. Patrick O'Brian's words allow me to feel I'm aboard a Napoleonic era sailing ship with characters I consider dear acquaintances. And Wodehouse's comedies unfailingly elevate my humor with the antics of some hilarious upper crust English buffoons.

The prime ingredients are skilled authors and readers. Accept no phonies, which comes from "fawney: gilt brass rings used by swindlers."

www.ingramcontent.com/pod-product-compliance
Lightning Source LLC
Chambersburg PA
CBHW051821020726
47502CB00005B/1561